the surprising way to a stronger marriage

how the power of one changes everything

Michael & Amy
Smalley

Tyndale House Publishers, Inc.
Carol Stream, Illinois

The Surprising Way to a Stronger Marriage: How the Power of One Changes Everything

A Focus on the Family book published by Tyndale House Publishers, Carol Stream, Illinois 60188

Focus on the Family and the accompanying logo and design are federally registered trademarks of Focus on the Family, Colorado Springs, CO 80995.

TYNDALE is a registered trademark of Tyndale House Publishers, Inc. Tyndale's quill logo is a trademark of Tyndale House Publishers, Inc.

All Scripture quotations, unless otherwise indicated, are taken from *The Message* [paraphrase]. Copyright © by Eugene H. Peterson 1993, 1994, 1995, 1996, 2000, 2001, 2002. Used by permission of NavPress Publishing Group. Scripture quotations marked (NIV) are taken from the *Holy Bible, New International Version®*. NIV®. Copyright © 1973, 1978, 1984 by Biblica, Inc.™ Used by permission of Zondervan. All rights reserved worldwide. (www.zondervan.com). Scripture quotations marked (ESV) are from *The Holy Bible, English Standard Version®*, (ESV®), copyright © 2001 by Crossway, a publishing ministry of Good News Publishers. Used by permission. All rights reserved.

Cover design: Stephen Vosloo
Cover photo: Mirror and checkered background copyright © L. Lema/PhotoLibrary. All rights reserved.

People's names and certain details of their stories have been changed to protect the privacy of the individuals involved. However, the facts of what happened and the underlying principles have been conveyed as accurately as possible.

The use of material from or references to various Web sites does not imply endorsement of those sites in their entirety.

Library of Congress Cataloging-in-Publication Data
Smalley, Michael.
  The surprising way to a stronger marriage / Michael and Amy Smalley. – 1st ed.
    p. cm. – (A focus on the family book)
  ISBN 978-1-58997-560-6 (alk. paper)
  1. Marriage—Religious aspects—Christianity. I. Smalley, Amy. II. Title.
  BV835.S558 2010
  248.8'44—dc22
                          2010014293

Printed in the United States of America
1 2 3 4 5 6 7 / 16 15 14 13 12 11 10

To David and Pauline

*After 50 years of marriage and still sweethearts,
you may never have written a book—but you have lived a
love story greater than anything we could ever write about!*

contents

acknowledgments

Thank heavens for the staff at Focus on the Family that made this little book possible! There is not enough space to thank everyone who has helped us. But we do want to write a special thanks to John Duckworth and Larry Weeden, two incredibly gracious, patient, and loving editors! You two believed in our book and allowed us the space to get it done.

To Cami Heaps, and the entire team of Author Relations and Product Marketing, thank you as well. We appreciate your vision for our book and your creativity in getting the message clearly worded!

is this book for you?

We want to be perfectly clear on the intended audience for this book.

The Surprising Way to a Stronger Marriage is for those who struggle with common issues that prevent the kind of intimacy most couples desire. It is *not* intended for anyone in an abusive marriage.

If any of the following is part of your marriage, you may be in an abusive relationship:

- physical abuse such as hitting or shoving
- verbal abuse including character assassination or threats of violence or other physical harm (simply yelling at each other is not necessarily verbal abuse; but when the language becomes threatening and violent, it is)
- a spouse with a serious personality disorder as diagnosed by a psychiatrist, medical doctor, or psychologist
- criminal activity
- drug or alcohol addiction
- serial infidelity, meaning that a spouse is having multiple affairs

This book is about taking personal responsibility in your marriage. But personal responsibility won't look the same for someone struggling with abuse as it will for someone facing irritations and disappointments. We would never recommend putting yourself or other family members in danger by remaining in an environment where abuse is taking place. Safety is your main concern when dealing with the issues we've just mentioned.

This book is for the vast majority of couples who do not face abuse—or other complex and dangerous problems that need the intervention of the police or a professionally trained counselor.

you've got the power

Their faces were filled with anguish as they approached us after one of our sessions at a marriage seminar. They wanted to smile, but years of unhappiness and regret had taken their toll on them. We saw their desperation, but we couldn't have been more surprised by what the husband said first.

"Can you fix this marriage in 30 seconds or less?"

Wow! We would like to fancy ourselves as talented marriage consultants. But this guy was asking for a miracle, and he was serious. *Thirty seconds or less? Are you kidding?*

Then it hit us, like Mike Tyson hitting Michael Spinks, and we came up with a reply.

"You want to fix your marriage in 30 seconds or less? Then start with changing yourself and decide to be a loving, supportive, active, and growing husband."

Not surprisingly, he didn't take to our answer.

This guy is like a lot of people in our culture. You might say we live in the land of the irresponsible and the home of the no-fault divorce; the demise of our relationships is the proof.

the power of one

When it comes to marriage, it's about time we all start growing up. Being an adult doesn't mean things become easier; in fact, it means things become more difficult.

That's because we, as adults, are responsible for our own actions and feelings. We can no longer play the victim's role as we may have done when we were children. Instead, we must start assuming the freedom and power we have in Christ if we belong to Him—which is the surprising way to a happier marriage.

I (Amy) remember a couple I worked with. Both spouses were committed Christians. Parents of small children, they volunteered in their church. Yet something was missing.

This couple and I worked through a Marriage Restoration Intensive (MRI), a sharply focused effort to rescue relationships in trouble.[1] Both mates learned about communication, conflict resolution, boundaries, effective time-outs, validation, love languages, and more. Yet there was something about the wife that seemed to hold her back. I could tell her spirit wasn't open to her husband. I cry every time I think of them because they struggled and struggled.

Taking responsibility takes time and energy, but it's surprisingly simple.

The wife knew something was wrong, but didn't know what. Was she depressed? Did she not have enough faith? Or was there something wrong with her husband?

The answer didn't come right away. But slowly the clouds lifted in their lives. Today their children still have a mom and dad who are together.

So what made the difference?

They both wrestled with their own issues. But the change really began when the husband took responsibility and made the first move.

He took the lead in giving her so much unconditional love it humbled me. He dug so deep to try to find her, he became bloodied and bruised along the way, but he found her. He wasn't a doormat; he drew boundaries when needed. But he gently offered his love over and over again. God did an amazing thing in their lives. Slowly she began to open up.

One day the husband contacted me, almost holding his breath for fear his wife might run away again. He could see that she was trying, that she was responding. This is an excerpt from an e-mail I got from him:

> Vulnerability and honesty have freed her from her cage that had grown so dark and so deep. Amy, I could have never imagined the beauty of the woman that had become locked in that box—beauty you could see. I often wish that you were right around the corner so that you could step into our family for a moment and see how God has used you. . . . I am still truly amazed in God's grace; He spared our family from destruction. He restored freedom and love.

Are you willing to fight the same fight? God is. He's willing to look you squarely in the eye and give you the wisdom you seek to draw you closer to your spouse. Taking responsibility takes time and energy, but it's surprisingly simple.

why are you here?

One of our favorite first lines when working with a couple is, "What brings you in today?" We're not the first people to ask this question, but it does have special meaning for us.

"What brings you in today?" often reveals the heart of many people's issues. Their response to this question tells us a lot about how successful they'll be in getting helped. If they start reciting a long list of complaints about each other, we know we're in a battle.

But the problem with their marriages—and yours, we believe—is not a list of grievances. It's how much each spouse is willing to take responsibility for those problems. Issues are just issues.

Often couples are stressed out because neither mate is willing to do the right thing—unless the other does it first. Or one spouse wants to work on the marriage while the other has "checked out" long before the couple reaches our door.

There is hope for both! Whether you're in marital limbo, crisis, or growth, God has a plan for you. We believe it includes releasing you from captivity (Isaiah 42:7) and freeing you to live a life worthy of your calling (2 Thessalonians 1:11).

When your own growth—not changing your spouse—is your goal, you won't fail. God will never leave you nor forsake you (Deuteronomy 31:6), even if a spouse does.

What brings you to reading this book today? Are you frustrated? Does your spouse not meet your needs as you'd like? Do you feel alone, rejected, or disconnected? Has life turned out to be one hugely disappointing experience after another?

It's an important question, so be careful with your answer. If you begin your reply with "my spouse" or "my child" or "my boss," you're not ready for the following pages. In fact, they might even rock the very core of your being.

This book is not about what your spouse must do so that you can enjoy a satisfied and happy marriage. It's about learning what *you* can do to help create an environment where a satisfied and happy marriage is possible.

does it really take two?

We are not slaves to our circumstances. We have options. The driver ahead of us doesn't force us to blow up at him when he cuts us off. Every reaction we display is our choice. We decide whether or not we're going to be upset, sad, frustrated, mad, or hurt.

We can control our own emotions. People, places, and things do not "make" us unhappy. We choose to feel unhappy as a result of what happens around us. We'll address this concept later, but it's important to note at the beginning of this book that you can choose how you respond to events.

True, you can't control what happens to you at the hands of other people. If you catch your spouse in an affair, your initial reaction will come from your gut. It's only natural. We're not talking about controlling that fear or frustration when faced with hardships or heartache. We're talking about controlling how you move forward and respond to tough circumstances.

If someone says something mean to me (Amy), it's natural for me to feel hurt—at first. But if I go home and take out my hurt on my kids or husband, that's my fault. If I lose sleep that night because I'm still ruminating over what happened, that's also my fault.

The old saying that it takes two to save a marriage isn't necessarily so. We've seen marriages experience the warmth and grace God intended because one spouse decided to make a change. That almost always results in the marriage—or any relationship for that matter—undergoing real change, usually in a positive direction.

one man who wouldn't give up

Authors Joe White and Lissa Johnson tell this story:

> When the tsunami rolled over Banda Aceh, Indonesia on December 26, 2004, truck driver Mustafa Kamal was far from home. He returned to find his wife, three daughters, and brother had vanished.
>
> Kamal stubbornly refused to believe his little girl, five-year-old Rina Augustina, was dead. Haunted by visions of her, the anguished father searched everywhere. He went from street to street, building to building, day after day.
>
> On January 26, 2005 the Associated Press reported the result of Kamal's month-long search. A powerful, moving photograph documents the moment that father and daughter were

reunited, thanks to the efforts of the Save the Children organization. When Rina spotted her daddy, she ran into his arms.

Kamal screamed, "By the grace of God! I knew you were alive! I knew it!" Then he added, "My precious little one. I did not give up. I kept looking."[2]

That dad was relentless.

He never gave up, never stopped hoping, never quit.[3]

That father also exercised the power of one. He took personal responsibility even if he had to do it alone.

The power of one is the way to many goals, including a stronger marriage. You can't just hope that your spouse does the work that you need to do. If you want your relationship to be better, then be better yourself. You have tremendous influence over a relationship when you focus your energy on being the kind of person you want your spouse to be.

getting results

What can you do to make a difference in your marriage?

We wish we could develop a magical pill to make your bond the absolute best, but we can't. What we *can* do is show you how to change and how to use the power of your change to make a positive impact on your relationship.

The old saying that it takes two to save a marriage isn't necessarily so.

Does this book guarantee a happy marriage? No. There are no guarantees, and anyone who tries to sell you one is a liar. But if you take the time to respond in as healthy a way as you can, you will change. When you change *you*, you change the way you move as a couple. When you decide not to engage in the unhealthy reactions of the past, you push your marriage in a better direction.

As we once wrote in *The DNA of Relationships*, God created all of us for relationships. That's good news for those who want to be closer to a spouse. When we start behaving well toward others, how will they respond? Will they get mad because we're treating them so well? Probably not.

More than likely, your spouse will respond in kind. He or she will treat you well because he or she is being treated well. It's the results of the Golden Rule!

Loving your spouse to the best of your ability ends up positively. Even if it takes time, hang in there and keep learning how to do the right thing. This book is about doing the right thing.

The more you know about what the right thing *is* in various situations, the better your marriage will be. That's why, toward the end of this book, we give you "Surprising Solution Scenarios." These are everyday examples of how to apply the lessons you've learned.

You'll also find a Study Guide at the back of the book. You can use it for personal reflection, discussion with your spouse, or group learning. This guide highlights the most important concepts we hope you'll get from each chapter.

today is the first day of the rest of your marriage

You are now ready to begin *The Surprising Way to a Stronger Marriage*. If you're reluctant to keep reading this book, remember there are forces that don't want your marriage to succeed. Resist! Keep moving forward and keep learning everything you can to make yourself a better lover, wife, husband, father, or mother.

With that in mind, let's start with a simple prayer:

Dear heavenly Father,

Please forgive me for the wrongs I've committed against You and against my marriage [feel free to pray about any specific problems God brings to mind]. I ask for Your protection as I read this book. If there is anything that would distract me from the truth, I ask that You keep it away. Help me keep an open heart and an open mind to Your will. I want Your goals accomplished in my life and my marriage. Amen.

You don't have to wait for your spouse to fix your marriage. Start doing it yourself. Experience the life-changing freedom of taking action—even if your mate doesn't seem ready to lend a hand.

when the truth
is hard to swallow

You may not want to hear what we're about to say in this chapter.

Before we say it, please understand that our pleasure and burden is loving couples in crisis. Our hearts ache to know that you probably are suffering. The hurt you feel is real, and we are so sorry you are going through this pain. We hope this book will help you prepare for, grow from, and mature through these trials.

Sometimes it's difficult to admit that even though you may not have control over your circumstances, you do have control over who you are in them. But focusing on who you are in the middle of painful situations is one of life's most challenging and rewarding experiences, especially if you're a Christ follower. It means letting go of what people—including your spouse—have done to you and concentrating on your attitudes or actions toward them.

Since none of us is perfect, none of us is completely innocent in marital conflict. There is always something we could have done better. This chapter is about helping you examine your own reactions so you can create an environment for your marriage to thrive. Examinations like that can be uncomfortable.

fault lines

John and Kris came to our Marriage Restoration Intensive (MRI) because of John's affair. Kris found out about the relationship when the woman involved with her husband called Kris to confess what was happening. What a phone call that must have been! Imagine having a woman who was sleeping with your husband call you out of the blue to confess because she was feeling guilty!

Kris was devastated, as any woman should be after getting a call from her husband's mistress. John and Kris initially tried to help themselves by reading several books, but their issues were too big to deal with alone. Eventually they called us and were scheduled to meet with me (Michael). I will never forget this intensive—for reasons you'll soon understand.

None of us is completely innocent in marital conflict.

The MRI was pretty normal through the first half-day. Kris was hurting, lashing out at John for having the affair. I gave her a chance to say what she needed to say; she really let him have it, and he sat there and took it for several hours. John was actually quite kind, and accepted responsibility for what he'd done. I could see how badly he felt.

After lunch I was ready to get Kris moving forward, wanting to help her begin the process of forgiveness. But Kris was uninterested in this part of the process. She couldn't let go of the fact that John had cheated on her.

Since it's not productive to let anyone get out of control during an intensive when sharing hurt feelings, I had to repeatedly interrupt Kris and help her find less aggressive ways to word how she felt. It got so bad after lunch that I began to get frustrated and impatient with her lack of forgiveness. Even though my wife has never cheated on me, I can understand how miserable an affair must feel; still, Kris was simply delivering one slashing statement after another.

I finally had to take drastic steps to help her regain control and to start thinking about her side of the affair. After all, there are always two sides to infidelity; rarely does a spouse have an affair when the marriage is extremely healthy. This doesn't mean an affair is a good way to respond to a broken marriage; it's an incredibly wrong and stupid way to respond, and only makes everything worse. But there's always the possibility that the unfaithful spouse wasn't the only person making mistakes.

I stopped Kris during one of her blasting statements toward John and asked her simply, "What was your part in this affair?"

As you can imagine, this was not a question Kris wanted to consider. For a moment I became the target of her anger and hurt. When she was done, I simply asked her again, "What was your part?"

She looked at me and said, "I had no part. This is all his fault!"

So I asked the question in a different way: "Have you ever done anything hurtful in your marriage toward John?"

"I don't know," she answered quickly.

That surprised me a little. Could she really be unaware of any mistakes she'd made? I looked at John and asked, "Has she ever hurt you in the past?"

He looked over at his wife. "Can I tell him about the affair you had?" he asked.

What? I truly did not believe what I was hearing. "Is it true that she had an affair?"

At this point Kris finally looked at me and said, "Yes, but that was almost two years ago!"

In her mind, apparently, the fact that she'd cheated on her husband 24 months ago was not as big a deal as her husband cheating on her more recently.

"So let me get this straight," I said. "I've been listening to you crush your husband for well over four hours because he had an affair. And this entire time you've not felt it was important to tell me that you have also had an affair?"

"I didn't think it was relevant," she said.

I finally understood why it was so hard for Kris to forgive John: His affair was only highlighting her own. Whether she wanted to admit it or not, she was just as guilty and messed up as he was.

Many of us are like Kris, denying our roles in our marital stories. But our shortcomings are *very* relevant to the relationship. When we can't see our own faults, our marriages suffer dramatically. When we fail to take ownership of our own problems, we usually end up blaming our spouses.

an inconvenient truth

We want to let you in on a little secret. We are all messed up!

One of our favorite things to do at the beginning of a seminar is to ask audience members to take a look at those sitting around them. Then we say, "Do you see all these people? They are sick people."

We do that because one excuse couples give for avoiding marriage enrichment seminars is that they don't want others to know their marriages may be in trouble. Let us ease your mind on this issue: Every marriage is in trouble at some point because every marriage is made up of broken, sinful individuals.

First Kings 8:46 puts it this way: "When they sin against you—and they certainly will; there's no one without sin! . . ." You might want to circle "no one without sin." The bad news is that we're all infected with this thing. It's made of our brokenness, heartache, mistakes, self-ishness, and disconnection from God.

The good news is that we're *all* infected by sin! We're all in this thing together. That means we can have compassion on each other, and offer each other grace and forgiveness. If no person is better than another, we all need to take ownership of our own junk. We can be gracious and merciful toward our spouse because we need and desire that same grace and mercy. Don't allow knowing about your sin to tear you down; instead, let it help you to be more humble and loving toward your spouse and others.

When we ignore our weaknesses, we can expect pride, impatience, and prejudice to follow. All three of these disconnect us from our spouse. Here's how:

- Pride separates us because we're too consumed by what we "deserve" to see what our spouse needs.
- Impatience draws us apart as our focus on our spouse's imperfections leaves us irritable and snappy.
- Being judgmental disconnects us because, frankly, who wants to hang out with someone who's predetermined what you mean, what you intend, and who you are?

Remember the last time you were proud, impatient, or judgmental toward your spouse? How did that go for you? This is a question we often ask couples at our Marriage Restoration Intensive; it helps people identify negative behaviors that need to change for the marriage to get better.

Asking yourself a question like "How did that work out for me?" helps you come to terms with destructive patterns in your life. If the answer is "Not very well," might we suggest taking a different path?

blaming's a shame

One more biggie that leads to disconnection is blaming others for our problems. When we blame our spouse for the breakdown of our marriage, we practically guarantee turmoil. Assigning fault pits one spouse against the other, setting the other person up to feel defensive and frustrated. It says, "If you hadn't done *this*, then I wouldn't have done *that*."

We've said it before and we'll say it again: We can't control what happens to us, but we can control how we respond. If we're going to end the blame game, this is a very important paradigm shift to make.

Let's say you're walking down the street. A total stranger approaches you and says, "What's wrong with you? Why aren't you acting like yourself today? You usually have such a nice smile on your face, but today you look like you swallowed a lemon. Are you PMS-ing or something?"

We hope nothing this obnoxious has actually happened to you.

But if it did, you couldn't keep this stranger from carrying out his verbal assault. You could, however, control how you respond.

When we blame people for our problems, we hand over the steering wheel of our lives to those we're blaming. We lose control over our lives. When both the problem and the solution are outside of you, you're powerless—the exact opposite of what you and we want you to be.

When we moved to Branson, Missouri, to work with my (Michael's) parents, I learned this lesson the hard way.

It's not that my parents are hard to get along with. When people learn who my father is, they often ask, "Was it difficult growing up with Gary Smalley as your dad?" The answer is always no, and it's a legitimate no. People assume that because my father is a famous marriage and family guy that he must have put high expectations on me and my siblings. I can honestly say that growing up in the Smalley home was awesome. My father and mother were loving, supportive, and encouraging. I think the key was in my father's transparency as an author and speaker. He had no desire to hide our family's flaws. In fact, he often encouraged us to make a mistake so he could have a new illustration! How's that for reverse psychology? I never felt pressured to be perfect, and I think we lived as normal a life as possible considering my dad sold tens of millions of books and videos.

So until age 18 I couldn't have been happier with my parents. Then I left for Baylor University and my relationship with them began to change. Things didn't suddenly become horrible between us; they were just different. Perhaps my parents had a difficult time making the transition from an adult-child relationship to an adult-adult one.

This became all too real when I moved to Branson with my wife and two kids. For seven or eight years I'd been living far away from my parents, raising my own family and getting educated in marriage and family counseling. Now, though, we were living practically next door to each other. Our first home in Branson was actually across the street from my parents' office.

This is when I learned what happens when you blame someone else for your own unhappiness.

To understand how it occurred, you must know that my mother is a cautious person. This is not necessarily bad. But when you live across the street and her office window provides a view of your home's front lawn, things can get touchy. When my wife would let our kids play in our yard, my mother would instantly call my office and report, "Hey, just wanted you to know that your kids are outside playing and I can't see Amy. Do you think that is safe?"

> **We can't control what happens to us, but we can control how we respond.**

Now that's a question loaded with a whole bunch of possible negative interpretations. *Are you saying that my wife is irresponsible? Are you hinting that I am a bad dad for letting my kids play outside without my wife watching? Are you saying we are bad parents and that you would make a far safer and better parent for our kids than we do?*

Every single day, Monday through Friday, my mother would call my office and ask if I thought it was okay to let my kids play outside without Amy. I let this daily call dictate my attitude toward my mother, father, wife, kids, friends, and even strangers on the street. I became almost unbearable to be around because I was so annoyed by my mother's fears.

The problem was that I gave control of my emotions and well-being to my mother. Essentially, I said to myself that I could only be happy if my mother stopped calling and harassing me about my kids playing in the front yard. I got cranky, irritable, and frankly, almost rude in my attitude toward my parents. That's right, I said *parents.* Even though my father wasn't doing the calling, I was mad at him for marrying my mother!

After several months of struggling with my parents and regretting my move to Branson, it was as if the Holy Spirit spoke to me like the thunder from a west Texas rainstorm. I can vividly remember the first thought God seemed to put in my head: *Am I really a bad parent?*

The problem, I began to realize, wasn't the fact that my mother was calling and asking if it was okay for my kids to play outside without Amy. It was the fact that when my mother asked this question I felt like a failure as a parent. The calls seemed to raise the possibility that I was not capable of raising my kids in an environment that would not kill them.

The surprising way to a stronger marriage looks at you every day— in the mirror.

I knew the answer to the question. I'd been in charge of these two kids for over five years, and they were still alive! Surely this meant I wasn't as defective a parent as I'd thought. Then a second question entered my mind: *Who is stressed out about my kids playing in the front yard?* I knew the answer to this question, too. (I can't remember another time when I got two questions correct in a row!) It was my mother. She was the one who was stressed out about my kids, not me.

The surprising solution was to take personal responsibility for my reactions, to not take on my mother's issues, and to return them to her.

The next day when my office phone rang, the typical dread I felt at seeing that it was my mother's extension was no longer there. Answering with a smile, I said, "Hello, how can I help you?"

She went into her normal routine of asking if it was safe for the kids to be playing outside alone. This time I simply replied, "Actually, I'm totally fine with them playing outside in the front yard. But I want you to know, if it bothers you then please feel free to go over and watch them. That wouldn't bother Amy and me at all. In fact, we'd love for you to watch them when they play outside."

Silence.

Then, all of a sudden, my mother responded: "Well, I can't really do that right now because I'm busy. But thanks for the offer."

The calls began to slow—at first almost daily, then only weekly. Finally they stopped altogether!

Once I returned my mother's issues to her, she tired of calling me because it meant she would have to do something about her fear. Her fear lost its power because she realized it wasn't bad enough to stop her from working. My attitude changed, too; I saw my mom and dad in a new light. No longer was I resentful and annoyed, but simply allowed them to be who they were.

taking the wheel

If you choose to ignore responsibility and give the steering wheel of your happiness and satisfaction to someone else, you run the risk of being miserable. Instead of feeling independent and secure, you'll feel dependent and insecure. The dependency comes because someone else has to do something different in order for you to feel happy. The insecurity comes because you don't know if that person will do what you need. You've officially lost control of your life and marriage.

When you don't accept personal responsibility, you can become . . .

- afraid to ever take a risk or make a decision.
- overwhelmed by disabling fears.
- unsuccessful at the enterprises you take on.
- emotionally or physically unhealthy.
- addicted to alcohol, drugs, food, gambling, shopping, sex, smoking, or work.

When you don't take personal responsibility in your marriage, you can become . . .

- resistant to vulnerability.
- unable to trust or to feel secure with your spouse.

- over-responsible and guilt-ridden in your need to rescue and enable your spouse.
- chronically hostile, angry, or depressed over how unfairly you think you've been treated by your spouse.

When you fell in love with your spouse, did you want these things in your marriage? Of course not.

But are these the things you're feeling now?

Only you know the answer.

The best news of all is that you can *change* the answer. You have the power to create an environment in your marriage that encourages your spouse to act in a healthy and loving way.

you're the problem—and the solution

Society is constantly downgrading personal responsibility. Just watch the news and you'll see people blaming others, the government, parents, and the weather for every sort of problem.

But here is the reality: *You* are both the problem and the solution.

If your attitude is that your spouse is the problem and the solution, good luck. You've tried that approach in the past. It didn't work then and it won't work now.

This book is about trying something different. Be the solution in your marriage. Be the kind of spouse you have always dreamed of having.

Jesus once said, "Here is a simple rule of thumb for behavior: Ask yourself what you want people to do for you; then grab the initiative and do it for them!" (Luke 6:31).

In other words, the surprising way to a stronger marriage looks at you every day—in the mirror.

3

"it's not my fault!"

Shouldn't marrying the son of a famous Christian marriage expert be a good thing? I (Amy) thought it was the last hard decision I'd have to make in my life. I believed Michael knew everything about relationships because of his dad. I truly thought life was going to be a downhill glide from our wedding forward.

I couldn't have been more wrong, or more naïve.

I'm not being mean—just honest. After one month of marriage, Michael and I found ourselves at a place where divorce felt like an option. We were miserable. We couldn't see the light of day through our constant fighting and avoiding each other. I would yell and Michael would run away.

This seesaw of emotions made life miserable. We weren't far from having one of those "starter marriages" in which a young couple gets married and divorced in less than a year.

What was wrong with us?

I easily saw all the mistakes Michael was making, of course. But since this is a book about taking personal responsibility, I guess I should stick to how I was hurting the marriage and contributing to the misery.

After all, my sin may look a little different from Michael's, but it's still sin. In this case, blaming was part of mine. When things went wrong in our marriage it was easy to look across the room and focus on Michael's infractions. But the reality was that we both were doing unproductive things. By focusing on Michael's brokenness, I put him down with blame and elevated myself with pride.

One of the most unhealthy things I used to say was, "I wouldn't be so angry if you wouldn't . . ." Another way to say this was, "You make me angry! I don't want to be angry, but you keep messing up!"

I'd convinced myself that I was a victim of Michael's imperfections. I truly believed I was right to get upset because Michael was making mistakes left and right. If Michael would only behave, I would not have to yell or get upset. In my mind, I was actually being forced to "express myself with intensity" (yell) at Michael. It was not my fault, but his!

Blaming sabotages the power of one— and your chance for a happier marriage.

Blaming Michael meant I felt less responsible for our bad marriage. The problem was that the relief I felt only seemed to last for a little while; then I felt the deep disconnection between us.

I was equally at fault for what was going on in our marriage. I was not a victim of Michael's sins; I was a victim of my own.

When we say "It's not my fault!" we start blaming. In this chapter we want to show how blaming sabotages the power of one—and your chance for a happier marriage.

excuses, excuses

Who was the first spouse to blame his mate? Adam.

He'd just been caught eating the fruit God had told him not to eat. Adam's response to God was one of the greatest examples of blaming ever recorded: "The Woman you gave me as a companion, she gave me fruit from the tree, and, yes, I ate it" (Genesis 3:12).

What an awesome specimen of blaming! Eating the forbidden fruit was the first mistake man ever made, followed by another— choosing to blame God and Eve! Very little has changed since then.

Instead of taking responsibility for his action, Adam actually accused God of being the real culprit behind Adam's own disobedience. It wasn't enough for Adam to simply pass blame on to his wife; he also tried to get out of trouble by pointing a finger at God: "If You hadn't made this woman, I would never have eaten that fruit. I don't want to blame You, God, I'm just saying . . ."

As Mike Golic of ESPN's *Mike and Mike in the Morning* radio show would say, "Just stop it!"

pride of the blamers

Why doesn't blaming work? Why did it hurt us during our first six months of marriage? Because blaming disconnects us from God and others. Blaming is a reflection of our pride.

Stopping the blame game means humbling ourselves, as Ben Reaoch of Pittsburgh's Three Rivers Grace Church notes. Reaoch writes, "Making excuses is arrogant and foolish. It's a proud way of trying to justify our actions and pacify our guilty consciences. And it keeps us from humbling ourselves before God to repent of *our* sins and seek His forgiveness."[1]

Pride prevents us from seeing the truth in our marriage. But as Jesus said in John 8:31-32 (NIV), "If you hold to my teaching, you are really my disciples. Then you will know the truth, and the truth will set you free."

Sometimes the most well-meaning but hurting people seek their own "truth" and it sets them "free"—often free to divorce their spouse. But God wants us to hold to His teachings first; as we fear and know Him, His truth is revealed. We need to humble ourselves before Christ, walk in obedience, and *then* ask what steps to take in our relationships.

"you're just dysfunctional"

Blaming your spouse for being "dysfunctional" won't fly, either. In fact, it can be ridiculous, considering you're probably just as messed up.

We believe there are two kinds of people in this world: those who are "normally dysfunctional" and those who are "specially dysfunctional." Notice that neither group is free from dysfunction. There are just different levels of it.

Normal dysfunction is, well . . . like you and us (we hope). We're talking about people trying to make their way in the world and trying to do the right thing.

Specially dysfunctional people are those affected by serious personality disorders—in the U.S., an estimated 10-15 percent of the population.[2] (And we are not sharing this information with you so you will try to diagnose your spouse. If you think your mate truly has a personality disorder, you need to consult a doctor or psychiatrist who uses sophisticated tests and measurements.)

The point of "normally dysfunctional" and "specially dysfunctional" is that we are all fallen, imperfect individuals.

It doesn't strengthen your marriage to blame God or others for your actions. When you take full responsibility for how you respond to people and circumstances, you are humbling yourself before God and man.

We give marriage the best chance of succeeding when we create an environment in which it can. As Abraham Lincoln said, "Most folks are as happy as they make up their minds to be." This is not meant to dismiss any pain or trial you are going through; it means *you can make it through.*

doing what comes naturally

If blaming doesn't work, why does it feel so good?

We deal with this issue when couples in crisis come to our Marriage Restoration Intensive program. They usually come in with an attitude that says, "This is what my spouse has done wrong."

There are three main reasons why people love to blame their spouse for a broken marriage:

1. It comes quite naturally to us (see Genesis 3:12).
2. It makes us feel better about ourselves.
3. It takes the focus off our own sinfulness.

We've already discussed how blaming is a natural reaction to sin. Because God created us with the freedom to choose, we can choose poorly. Blaming is a poor choice in any situation. It only leads to further problems and heartache.

Blaming makes us feel better about ourselves because we can use it to justify our response to being wronged. When our spouse does something we don't like and we choose to react poorly, we might feel guilty about our poor reaction. But if we blame our spouse for our bad reaction, we don't have to feel as bad.

Unfortunately, this doesn't last very long. That's because it's a flawed response. It actually leads to feelings of bitterness and unforgiveness. The cycle of blaming doesn't improve our situation; it always makes it worse.

It also leads to being judgmental. When we blame our spouse for the problems in our marriage, it takes our eyes off our own sinfulness and focuses them on the sinfulness of our mate. If you've read what Christ said in the New Testament, you know that being judgmental is the last thing you want to be:

> Do not judge, or you too will be judged. For in the same way you judge others, you will be judged, and with the measure you use, it will be measured to you.
>
> Why do you look at the speck of sawdust in your brother's eye and pay no attention to the plank in your own eye? How can you say to your brother, "Let me take the speck out of your eye," when all the time there is a plank in your own eye? You hypocrite, first take the plank out of your own eye, and then you will see clearly to remove the speck from your brother's eye.
>
> Do not give dogs what is sacred; do not throw your pearls

to pigs. If you do, they may trample them under their feet, and then turn and tear you to pieces. (Matthew 7:1-6, NIV)

better than blaming

Blaming doesn't work because it keeps the cycle of sin spiraling out of control. Jesus' teaching in Matthew is so important: When we spotlight the sin in our spouse, we're merely highlighting our own! In fact, Jesus goes so far as to say that our sin is worse than that of the person we're putting under the microscope.

We can't waste valuable energy focusing on what's wrong with our spouse. We need to save it to use on our own problems. The more energy we use trying to change our spouse, the less energy we have to deal with our own stuff.

So what's the alternative to blaming?

When something's gone wrong in a marriage, the most helpful attitude to take is to ask yourself this question:

How could I have handled that better?

No matter what's going on in a marriage, we can always find something we could have done better.

By focusing on your spouse's mistakes, you make the marriage less happy—and yourself more vulnerable to the consequences of blaming. Try asking yourself, *What could I have done differently? How do I need to change to make this marriage better?*

> *Try asking yourself, What could I have done differently?*

When you can ask these questions, you're on your way to a happier relationship.

Whether you're 95 percent or 5 percent to blame for what's going wrong in your marriage, taking ownership of your part will help the other person to own his or hers.

It's not about percentages and blame. It's about doing the right thing.

getting off the defense

We wanted a powerful illustration about defensiveness to start off this chapter. This time we didn't have to scour the Web, browse books of anecdotes, or even "borrow" one from somebody else. Just this morning God dropped the perfect illustration into our lives.

My (Michael's) dear friend Casey McKown came to drive our family to the airport today. We were heading to Phoenix, Arizona, to speak at a conference, and the kids were joining us. When my wife finally came outside to get in the car, it happened.

Casey and I were standing at the front of my Honda Odyssey as Amy passed us to climb into the van. Walking by, she made a comment only a wife would make: "Casey, do you see the damage Michael did to the front bumper when he hit a tire yesterday on the freeway?"

My reaction was swift and immediate: "*What?*"

I was upset for two reasons. First, I didn't even know the bumper was messed up, which only proves what an unmanly man I really am. Second, that was totally unfair!

As Amy knelt down by the damaged front bumper, she pointed out the massive black mark and the fact that the side of the bumper was now detached from the vehicle. Again she highlighted how I'd hit the tire on the freeway.

I did what any normal human being does when getting unfairly blamed—I got defensive! "And by 'hit a tire on the freeway,'" I retorted, "do you mean a car swerved in front of us, cutting us off, and blew a tire which then flew across the ground at blinding speed and smacked into our front bumper?"

What did I get for my brilliant argument? A simple, yet profound "Nope, you hit it." Amy got in the car with a wry smile, the kind that says, "Gotcha!"

As I was preparing my "you're not allowed to blame me" speech, God quietly reminded me that my defensiveness was getting me overly worked up. Amy was clearly messing with me, and I was allowing my pride to cause me to react poorly.

This is why defensiveness is so unhelpful in relationships.

the defense department

Defensiveness is a person's attempt to resolve a problem through arguing, explaining away, or being combative. When we argue with someone about the facts surrounding a circumstance, we're being defensive. When conflict occurs, the "remembered" facts of the situation are rarely accurate. It never does us any good to argue facts with our spouse—or anyone else, for that matter. Discussing the facts only causes defensiveness in the person we're arguing with!

It doesn't matter whether you meant to hurt your spouse; your spouse is hurting.

Explaining away is another popular form of being defensive. It doesn't initially appear argumentative or combative, but this could not be further from the truth.

Take, for example, a couple we saw recently in one of our Marriage Restoration Intensives. When we asked the wife what it would take to get her marriage from a 3 to a 10 (1 being horrible and 10 being great), she said, "It would be nice if we could spend more time together at home just hanging out and not working on the computer."

The wife's voice was calm as she shared her need, but the husband's reaction was swift. "What do you mean, 'spend more time together at home'? When I'm home all you seem to want to do is sit on the couch and watch your favorite shows. How can that be spending time together? I would love to spend more time together at home, but it is not my fault this isn't happening!"

See the breakdown in communication, and the defensiveness? The wife obviously felt they weren't spending much time together at home. Her definition of spending time together was clearly different from her husband's, but he reacted poorly by getting upset and defensive. The husband took her need as a direct assault on him, a claim that he was at fault. He fought back by trying to explain away his wife's opinion.

You know the drill. You get accused of something; you feel that if you could only convince your spouse about the inaccuracy of her opinion or experience, things would get better. But things don't get better—ever—when we try to explain away our spouse's feelings or needs.

Defensiveness causes unhappiness and a communication breakdown because it escalates the negative emotions we're already experiencing. Have you ever noticed your spouse calming down as a result of being defensive? Probably not.

So why do we keep doing it? Because we're not taking responsibility for our emotions and choices. Defensiveness is a direct result of a lack of taking responsibility. Who wants to be told his or her feelings and needs are inaccurate or wrong? No one.

the offense of defensiveness

We choose to react defensively even though we know it's not going to help resolve the conflict. We've found three reasons why people tend to get defensive:

1. *We get defensive because we're sinful.*

We've discussed this before, and there's no escaping it. Our point is not to make you feel bad about your sin, but to encourage you to be humble and understand your spouse's needs and feelings. Our sin doesn't define us; God does. Being created in God's image gives us tremendous value. Yet our tendency to do the wrong thing does affect how we behave.

2. *We get defensive because we want to prove we're right or our spouse is wrong.*

How many arguments have you gotten into with your spouse because you wanted to prove something? Does it feel good when your spouse or someone else tries to invalidate your feelings or needs? Probably not.

Getting into a "who's right" or "who's wrong" conversation is never a good thing. The conflict will only get worse. You'll never come together as a team if you are constantly on opposing sides, like lawyers in a courtroom.

3. *We get defensive because we feel bad that something we did was misunderstood.*

This reason for defensiveness can be the hardest to overcome. It seems unfair to be punished for something we didn't do intentionally.

It sounds so logical to explain away our spouse's hurt: "If only he would listen to me and let me explain what I meant, he would feel better." But our spouse doesn't feel better after we've tried to explain away the hurt, does he?

> *It's not enough to stop being defensive; you need to replace past behaviors with new ones.*

Unintended pain is still pain. We must come to grips with this concept. It doesn't exonerate you in a court of law, for example, if you accidentally kill someone. There's a term for this kind of crime: manslaughter. It means you are guilty of a crime even though you didn't mean to commit it. Maybe you were being reckless or were distracted for only a second; but if you kill someone you will typically get punished whether you meant to or not.

The same is true relationally. It doesn't matter whether you meant to hurt your spouse; your spouse is hurting. Take on the hurt and listen to how you can repair it. This is a great way to take personal responsibility, and a simple way to help your marriage succeed.

the defense rests

Since defensiveness doesn't work, how can you start responding differently to your spouse's hurt or unmet expectations?

Here are six responses that are more constructive.

1. *Validate.*

We'll talk more about validating in a later chapter. For now, you need to know that it's the exact opposite of being defensive. Validation shows that your spouse is more important to you than proving her wrong or proving yourself right. Validation is all about putting your own opinions and attitudes to the side in order to say, "Your feelings matter to me, and I want to understand them."

2. *Listen.*

Instead of being defensive, try listening. When you listen, it sends a message to your spouse that he or she is important and worth keeping your mouth closed for. Listening is such an easy way to help calm someone down—as long as you are listening well.

Listening well involves eye contact, positive attitude, and good posture. Rolling your eyes and letting out sigh after sigh is not a good way to listen. Focus all your attention on your spouse and see how things start to calm down.

Being a great listener is like being a great counselor. There's an entire school of therapy called Rogerian psychology, founded by Carl Rogers, that bases everything on the ability of the counselor to simply listen and reflect what the client is saying.

3. *Ask questions.*

Instead of being defensive, ask questions. Too few couples seem to understand the art of simply making queries.

Open-ended questions can be a powerful tool in calming down

your spouse. They sound like this: "It feels like I've done something to upset you; can you help me understand what I did?"

The two of us use questions all the time when our feelings get hurt or when we're feeling defensive. They're a nice way to bring the discussion to a healthier, more rational level.

4. *Allow your spouse to have his or her own opinions.*

You and your spouse can't possibly agree on everything. Michael and I are so different in personality and background that we find ourselves constantly disagreeing over meaningless things.

It's okay to have differing opinions on many issues like food, fun, and romance. The trick is to allow for differences and to recognize what truly matters and what doesn't.

Many people seem to feel their opinions are superior to their mate's; they're only too glad to highlight what they see as their spouse's faulty thinking. We need to allow our mate to have a different opinion. There are times when we can reach a win-win solution, but also times when we need to accept our mate's right to another point of view.

> **You have more influence than you imagine when it comes to affecting your spouse for the better.**

5. *Get off the facts and onto the feelings.*

Defensiveness is rarely about facts. We get defensive because we're hurting. We're hurting because a button has been pushed—a button like feeling rejected, controlled, powerless, like a failure, and disconnected. For a more thorough explanation of buttons, see our Web site at www.smalley.cc/marriage-assessments/the-core-fear-test.

Ask yourself this: *Has focusing on facts ever calmed down my spouse in the past?* We doubt it. Discussing facts with your spouse during a confrontation usually is pointless, especially when you're feeling defensive.

Nothing good is going to come out of such a discussion, so we need to take the topic from facts to feelings. If you're intimidated about sharing feelings, download our list of "hot buttons" from the Web site (using the "help" button) and use it to help you identify what's really bothering you.

6. *When you can't "stop it," stop talking.*

Calling a time-out when things aren't going well is a healthy step. Just remember that as soon as you call a time-out, the clock starts ticking for a time-in.

When you feel defensive, ask for a break. Take time to calm down and get an attitude adjustment; prayer works best. After you calm down and (hopefully) God has humbled you, you'll be in a better frame of mind to talk again.

the best defense

Defensiveness is destructive and only makes things worse. Stopping it begins with a decision; you have to decide that defensiveness doesn't work.

Once you've made that decision, the next step is to replace the negative behavior with something more constructive. It's not enough to stop being defensive; you need to replace past behaviors with new ones.

In the same way, it's not enough to hate the negative things going on in your relationship. That's why the rest of this book is about helping you replace the negative patterns that have crept into your marriage. Each chapter explains a different way to respond to your spouse. The guidelines are simple, but the improvements they can bring may surprise you.

Maybe you're reading this book and feeling wiped out. You're hoping this book will provide a miracle for your marriage. Our book can help, but the key is understanding that *you* are the miracle! You have more influence than you imagine when it comes to affecting your spouse for the better.

Remember the Golden Rule, Jesus' instruction in Luke 6:31. Be the person you want others to be.

Be the change. The healthier—and less defensive—you are, the better the chances that your marriage will succeed.

Don't wait for your spouse to get on the healthy marriage train. Jump on it yourself and watch what happens. That train is like a party! Your spouse may well hear all the happy noises coming from those passenger cars and want to jump on it with you.

5

you don't have
to be a victim

Have you ever been utterly humiliated by your spouse in public? I
(Amy) got to experience this at the hands of my husband in February
of 2009.

I love this illustration because it's one of the times where I actually handled myself correctly—which is more than I can say for
Michael. Usually I'm the "escalator" and the one needing to apologize
for mishandling myself during a conflict. But the dysfunction falls directly on Michael's shoulders this time!

Birthday number seven was coming up for David, our youngest
child. David loves routine, and for the third year in a row he wanted
to have his party at a place near our house called Pump It Up. A great
venue for kids, it's filled from floor to ceiling with these awesomely in-
flated trampolines, slides, and obstacle courses.

We downloaded party invitations so we could print, fold, and
hand them out to all the kids in David's class. Michael had the idea
of making custom changes to the invitation, using some graphic design programs he's learned over the years. Thrilled by his suggestions,
I gave him the thumbs-up. He made the additions, and I was quite excited about what we'd done to the card.

Unfortunately, this would be the last time I'd feel any kind of positive emotion about this invitation.

The following morning I had to leave early for work, and was gone before my kids even awoke. Michael was in his office putting the fin-ishing touches on the card when David walked in and excitedly asked what he was doing. Michael showed him the card on the computer screen; David loved it!

Then our son asked a question: "Daddy, can you put on the card what I want for my birthday?"

Sounds like an innocent question, doesn't it? But the answer Michael gave will haunt me for the rest of my days.

"Of course!" he said. "Daddy can put whatever you want on this card!"

So our son asked Michael to put on the invitation—the one that was going to be handed to every mother in David's class—"David is requesting CASH for his birthday present."

I still have a hard time believing that Michael didn't even con-sider how this request could come across as inappropriate and rude. Alas, he did not.

Instead, he made the change, printed the cards, folded them up, and handed one to each kid in the class. It wasn't until later that day, when Michael was sitting under the big oak tree at David's school, that he wondered whether it might be weird to put such a request on a birthday invitation.

We choose our responses to demands, injustices, threats, and opportunities.

One of the moms in our son's class was sitting next to him under the tree. Michael leaned over and asked whether she had opened the invitation yet. She said no. He then asked her if it was weird to put David's request for CASH on the birthday invitation.

Her response was classic: "Oh, no. You did not put that on David's birthday card."

He said yes.

She asked if I knew what had been added to the card. He told her I had not seen the cards yet.

"Don't tell her," the mom warned.

We usually don't endorse keeping secrets, but Michael did feel that this secret had real implications for whether his life would be going on or ending. He was probably correct! If you're weeping in empathy for me, thanks!

The party came, and I was clueless about the invitation. I did wonder why all the moms were bringing envelopes rather than wrapped gifts. I even brought this to Michael's attention. It didn't bother me; I assumed the envelopes contained only birthday cards. I was actually pretty happy that the moms didn't feel obligated to bring David presents; he already had enough toys, and I told Michael so.

At this point in the story, I must allow Michael to interject his perspective, which he is itching to do:

Can you imagine my horror at the healthy attitude of my wife? Here I was, getting prepared to be lambasted, and she pulls out this statement! I could not believe my ears. I knew Amy was loving and gracious, but this was crazy! I already felt bad for what she was about to find out, but her attitude of graciousness at thinking no one was bringing any gifts only made my sickness worse.

I've said my piece. Amy can continue now.

Thanks for giving me permission, Sweetie.

Michael was quickly becoming aware of how much trouble his little invitation was about to get him into. And then it happened.

One of the moms, a good friend of ours, came right up to me with David's present. It was a nicely colored tin filled to the brim with coins. She was quite proud of her sarcastic moment and winked toward Michael, knowing full well that she was getting him into trouble!

She then handed me the invitation and politely said, "I was so thankful your husband let us all know what David wanted for his birthday present."

That was it. The secret was out.

I did what any wife would do in that moment. I whacked Michael on the arm, pulled him close to my lips, and whispered, "We'll talk about this later."

I did it! I actually controlled my emotions and put them on hold until we could finish David's party. Nothing is worse than ruining a party with a horrible fight. Knowing this, I actually made a decision to put off the discussion until we got home. I wanted to keep David's party intact—and the reality was that I did not *have* to respond with anger.

I had a choice, and so do you.

mr. powerless and mrs. fear

We all have a choice when it comes to our reactions. There are no victims in a healthy marriage, only two people totally responsible for their own emotions and responses.

We've already outlined why you don't want to be a victim in any relationship. Victims feel powerless and out of control. In reality, we're neither. We can choose how we respond to any circumstance or situation.

If we don't take control over our emotions and reactions, Mr. Powerless and Mrs. Fear will. If we don't take command of how we respond, the only choice we leave ourselves is powerlessness and fear.

One of the more important things we learned early in our marriage is that we don't *make* each other feel anything. This might sound impossible, but it's true. People, places, or things cannot make us feel or do anything. We choose our responses to demands, injustices, threats, and opportunities.

Second Corinthians 5:10 reads, "Sooner or later we'll all have to face God, regardless of our conditions. We will appear before Christ and take what's coming to us as a result of our actions, either good or bad." Notice that this verse says nothing about other people. It mentions only us. We will appear in front of Christ one day and take responsibility for how we handled ourselves while living on earth.

You might ask, *But what about the devil? Aren't we victims of his temptation and harassment?*

Evil is a real problem in everyone's life. In a sense, we are all victims of Satan's plot against mankind until Christ returns. But as 1 Peter 5:8-10 says:

> Keep a cool head. Stay alert. The Devil is poised to pounce, and would like nothing better than to catch you napping. Keep your guard up. You're not the only ones plunged into these hard times. It's the same with Christians all over the world. So keep a firm grip on the faith. The suffering won't last forever. It won't be long before this generous God who has great plans for us in Christ—eternal and glorious plans they are!—will have you put together and on your feet for good.

"Stay alert" is an active and personal statement to us. The devil would like nothing else than for us to be unaware of our power and ability to resist and defend ourselves from his attacks. Scripture is filled with references like this about taking responsibility for our lives.

With God's help, we can take control over protecting ourselves and responding to circumstances. I (Amy) easily could have freaked out at David's birthday party and really let Michael have it for humiliating me in front of my son's friends. But I did not *have* to freak out. I had a choice, and so do you.

Michael messed up the invitation, but that doesn't mean I had to lose control and handle myself in a destructive way. I did feel embarrassed, but I was strengthened by knowing that my emotional response was my choice. Michael did not control how I felt—I did.

time to take control

Your spouse does not *make* you feel anything. Your feelings are a direct result of your choices. If you choose to feel humiliated, distraught, or depressed, there is no one to blame but yourself.

We don't want to be insensitive to the hurt you may have experienced from a spouse—or from anyone else. We *do* want you to understand the control you have over what you feel and how you respond.

Are you going to allow someone else's errors to bring you down?

Your spouse and other people are going to continue sinning against you. There is no way to avoid it. Sin permeates this entire planet.

The question is, how are you going to respond to sin?

Are you going to allow someone else's errors to bring you down?

Or are you going to make a stand and choose to respond in a productive, loving—and even surprising—way?

6

letting God handle
the hard stuff

I (Michael) have struggled with my weight for more years than I care to admit. Sometimes I feel like my addiction to food is as intense as a person's addiction to heroin. Currently I am down 25 pounds and am developing what I like to call a "Lifestyle Revolution."

If you haven't noticed yet, the key word in the previous paragraph is "I." *I* have the weight problem and *I* am the one who needs help and encouragement to change.

For many years Amy and I were at odds about my weight issues. I am the luckiest man on earth to be married to her; I was so enamored when I first saw her that I actually became a male cheerleader (because she was a cheerleader) to get her to notice me and fall in love with me, too. So when I married Amy, I married the woman of my dreams!

But then we started having children. Each time Amy got pregnant she would relax her very healthy eating habits. I can remember driving to the ice cream store in the late evenings because Amy had cravings, and naturally I would buy something for her *and* something for me.

Three kids later, I was massively overweight. I probably averaged close to 25 pounds per kid. I know this sounds strange—a man claiming that having children caused him to gain weight—but it's true. What really bothers me, thinking back on those days, is that after

Amy would give birth, literally within two weeks she would be back to her pre-pregnant weight! It was totally unfair.

Once our third and final kid was born, I announced to Amy that I was finished putting on all her pregnant weight for her. I understand that her pregnancies were not at the root of my weight gain. But my expansion caused Amy a lot of frustration, as she now shares:

I (Amy) have never had a problem with being overweight. My problem was feeling pressure to be underweight. As a college cheerleader I felt it, especially when I heard guys talking about how hard it was to lift a certain girl. I never wanted to be "that girl."

I dealt with my desire to be lightest by eating very little. I don't believe I was ever anorexic, but felt a need to control my weight at an intense level. Watching Michael gain pounds at the beginning of our marriage was difficult. I didn't understand why he couldn't control his weight as I did. I tried to "help" by presenting health information, commenting on his sugar and fat intake, and criticizing and shaming him.

> **It was as if God said, "If you stop pushing so hard, maybe I can get through to him."**

For years we fought over eating habits. The more I tried to get Michael to eat better and exercise, the worse things got. I seemed to become a major hindrance to his losing weight.

I struggled with this issue for many years, trying to get him to change. But the problem only got more severe. Things would get ugly, with name-calling from both sides.

But one day God finally got through to me. He convinced me to use a different strategy to help Michael: backing off.

It was as if God said, "If you stop pushing so hard, maybe I can get through to him. He will always have an excuse if you keep opening your big mouth and messing everything up." (God seems to talk to me that way, perhaps because I need to be whacked upside the head sometimes.)

He also seemed to ask me this question: "How much 'anger weight' have you lost?"

God knew that was my biggest struggle. I thought about it and responded, "Maybe 10 to 15 pounds."

"And how much do you still need to lose?"

I felt like the biggest heel. "A lot."

"Then why don't you focus on that? Because I could tell you all the reasons why you need to lose anger weight."

It was true and I knew it. I went to Michael and said, "Oh, Michael, love of my life, I am so sorry for harping on your junk when I have just as much of my own. I will love you for as many days as we have together, and I will not allow myself to miss out a single day longer by focusing on your weight. Please forgive me."

What happened next? I'll let Michael explain:

Amy approached me with her new insight about my weight issues. I can vividly remember her releasing me to God for help with my struggle. Suddenly, once Amy handed me over to God, I had no one to blame for my weight problem but myself.

giving it to God

Ever tried to change something in your spouse? Maybe he or she is addicted to smoking, drinking, drugs, pornography, or lying, or resists a relationship with God. Whatever the problem is, trying to change it *for* your mate will only make it worse!

If you've tried that, how did it work for you? This is a question we love to ask audiences at our live events. *How did that work for you?*

The crazy thing about most people is that they keep doing the very things they've already proven to be unsuccessful. If you want things to improve in your marriage, do something different: Try handing over your spouse's issues to God.

We know this sounds incredibly clichéd, but it's completely necessary. (Remember, however, our disclaimer at the beginning of this book: We're not telling abused individuals to simply hand over the abuse to God and then stay in harm's way. Safety is your primary concern in an abusive marriage.)

Maybe you're getting ready to close this book and toss it in the trash. You're thinking, *I've tried that, giving it over to God. It did not work!*

But why give up on God? How long have you tried? One year? Five years? Fifteen? How much is enough time to allow God to change your spouse?

We know it's not easy to wait. And some things about your spouse may never change, which is why taking responsibility for your own reactions is so important. But we also believe we should never put a time limit on God. Unable to truly understand His plans, we must be patient with Him.

The Bible never gives us an "out" when it comes to relying on God. Where's the verse that says we can quit? God is a God of healing and restoration; our job is to get out of the way and allow Him to do His.

Consider 2 Timothy 2:24-26:

> God's servant must not be argumentative, but a gentle
> listener and a teacher who keeps cool, working firmly but
> patiently with those who refuse to obey. You never know
> how or when God might sober them up with a change of
> heart and a turning to the truth, enabling them to escape
> the Devil's trap, where they are caught and held captive,
> forced to run his errands.

If we hope for change, our interaction with our spouse must be gentle. Being cruel, rude, or critical with our mate is a losing formula. The fact that our spouse may be sinning against us doesn't justify sinning against him or her.

We can be sure, though, that God wants the best for us and our spouse. He is the most powerful agent of change:

> Don't become so well-adjusted to your culture that you fit into it without even thinking. Instead, fix your attention on God. You'll be changed from the inside out. Readily recognize what he wants from you, and quickly respond to it. Unlike the culture around you, always dragging you down to its level of immaturity, God brings the best out of you, develops well-formed maturity in you. (Romans 12:2)

When we struggle with the shortcomings of our spouse, we need to fix our attention on God. If we waste our energy by focusing on what's broken with our mate, we know how it will end—in futility.

Even if your spouse doesn't believe in God or is being resistant, God can still make an impact. He is much bigger than anyone who resists His influence and authority.

what would you like to change today?

What's your biggest complaint about your spouse? Is there anything constructive you can do with that complaint?

One of our mentors is Dr. Ed Laymance, counseling pastor at Lake Arlington Baptist Church in Arlington, Texas. He has a wonderful exercise he calls "flushing." We want to borrow the idea here without going into great detail (it might be called plagiarism if we did). The term *flushing* is so appropriate for what you need to do with issues against your spouse.

Take a moment and write out how you most want your spouse to change. Make sure to keep this list private; it would be cruel and extremely unfair to let your spouse see it. But on paper, let it all out and don't hold anything back.

Now take a few minutes to pray the following prayer aloud. Take the time to let it soak in by meditating on it and asking the Holy Spirit to show you how it applies to your life. Take a deep breath and rest in it.

> Lord, please forgive me for how I approach [spouse's name].
> I have been judgmental and impatient, and I'm sorry. I am
> handing over my spouse to You, God, right now. I am no
> longer in charge of [spouse's name]'s growth; I am handing
> it all over to You. I ask for patience, kindness, and mercy as
> [spouse's name] struggles through [add your spouse's strug-
> gles]. Give me Your heart as I deal with my spouse. Let Your
> will be done, and give me the insight to understand Your plan
> for our marriage. Amen.

This is a great first step in your process of letting go of the changes you want to see in your spouse. Your need for prayer is not over. Come back to this prayer as often as you need to. Allow time for God to work on your heart over whatever your spouse is struggling with.

your PIT crew

The next step is to build yourself a PIT Crew. This idea comes from our dear friend and prayer mentor Colin Millar, founder of Igniting Prayer Action. His official title is Prayer Strategist. We know that be-cause it's on his business card. Nothing gets past us!

Colin has a plan for developing a group of individuals who com-mit to praying for you in a specific way. That's important because so many of us are so isolated. We may go to church and pretend every-thing is okay when in fact we're going through major hurt and rejec-tion in our marriages and elsewhere.

We don't have to pretend any longer that everything is fine. Every-one is struggling through the same problems. No one is free from the curse of sin in this world, and we all suffer the consequences.

The point of a PIT (Personal Intercessory Team) Crew is to pray the purposes, promises, and plans of God "into, over, and through the life of the person" it serves. All this means is that you gather a group of individuals who commit to praying for you specifically. Intercessory prayer is praying for others. Your PIT Crew will ask for God's help in your marriage.

Colin outlines nine ways a PIT Crew functions. They include listening and praying for God's purposes in your life, functioning as crisis intercessors, hearing your requests, and resisting the urge to offer advice instead of prayer.

Who do you want on your PIT Crew? Choose only people who are committed to you and the marriage. The ability to respect your confidentiality will be important as well. Make sure crew members are strong in their faith; you want mature Christians on this team.

> **Whatever the problem is, trying to change it for your mate will only make it worse.**

Colin recommends that a crew should be made up of three to twelve people. If possible, they should meet in person or through a conference call once a month to pray for you. For information on how a PIT Crew might help your marriage, go to www.ignitingprayer action.org.

is your spouse in good hands?

It's important to hand over your spouse's issues to God. God, not you, can change your spouse if He chooses.

Once Amy released me to be worked on by God, I started the process of getting ready to eat and live in a healthier way. The key is that it was *my* work to be done.

As a spouse, you can be a great cheerleader. Just remember not to be the coach. A coach tends to control every aspect of a player's athletic life, but this doesn't work in a marital relationship. You are not your mate's boss.

If your spouse asks for your help, then by all means jump in there and assist. But you must be asked. Never assume that your spouse wants you coaching his or her life.

As a spouse, you can be a great cheerleader. Just remember not to be the coach.

Handing over your spouse to God is a process. It starts with your acknowledgment that it needs to happen. If you begin with a prayer like the one in this chapter and follow through with a PIT Crew, your chances of success will increase.

Why? Because it isn't easy to stop trying to change your mate. It takes prayer—and a community—to help release your spouse to God.

which way are you leaning?

What would be the hardest thing to forgive your spouse for?

A wife in one of our Marriage Restoration Intensives faced this issue. She was mad. And when we say mad, we mean she was ready to leave her marriage and barely agreed to even meet with us. When we greeted this couple in the lobby of our office, the flames of anger from her eyes nearly singed the hair off our heads!

What could have made this wife so angry? She and her husband had been married for just a few years and had recently welcomed their first child. How bad could things be? Apparently, pretty bad.

When we sat down in our office, the wife accused her husband of having an affair. For several minutes we listened to her feelings and tried to process her accusations. The details she was giving were sketchy—and, frankly, did not make a lot of sense.

Finally we asked with whom she suspected her husband was having this affair. That's when she said she'd discovered pornography on their home computer.

Aha! So the affair she was talking about was with a computer and watching porn. Her discovery had been pretty brutal—for both of them. Like many wives, she had never seen porn until accidentally finding it on that computer.

Now her story was beginning to make more sense. The husband remained quiet; he understood how mad his wife was, and didn't want to get in more trouble.

If you were the wife in this case, what would you do at this point? When something really hurtful has occurred, how do you respond?

Remember, this is a book about personal responsibility. No matter what happens in a marriage, we're always responsible for our own actions. We respond as victims or offenders. This chapter outlines what to do when you've been wronged—or have wronged your spouse.

leaning in

When something negative happens and you don't know what to do, *lean in*.

We define *leaning in* as being vulnerable with your spouse about your feelings and needs. Both parties are responsible to do this; but if you're the only one who's willing, start by yourself.

> **The flames of anger from her eyes nearly singed the hair off our heads!**

Leaning in works best when feelings aren't judged or criticized and solutions are carried out. If your spouse says, "I feel demeaned when _____ is said about me," then it's your responsibility to honor that feeling by repeating it back: "I understand you feel demeaned when _____ is said about you."

We take steps forward by not being defensive, as we've mentioned before. You can also step forward by simply engaging with your spouse. We know it's difficult to engage (or lean in) when your feelings get hurt. Our natural response is to lean *back* and wait for the offender to approach.

If you're hurt by your spouse's poor choices, you can lean in by . . .
- seeking understanding.
- allowing for imperfections (which doesn't mean what happened was okay or should continue).
- forgiving—giving up the right to revenge.

are you overreacting?

The couple we mentioned at the beginning of this chapter seemed headed for divorce. Is divorce the remedy if your spouse has looked at pornography? No.

Is looking at porn wrong? Yes. Porn turns people into objects, exploits them, encourages lust and selfishness, ignores God's intentions for sexuality, and leads to becoming insensitive to a spouse's needs. It is dangerous and highly addictive.

We challenged the wife to understand what her husband was doing with the porn. At first, traumatized by her discovery, she'd rushed to many conclusions. She assumed, for one thing, that he was watching porn all the time. This proved to be inaccurate. Once she calmed down enough to listen to his side of the conflict, she found that he had downloaded that free video clip over a year prior to her finding it. She verified this information by the date of the file on the computer. He'd looked at porn, but it may have been only three times since they'd gotten married. He was clearly not a "sicko," as his wife put it.

Could he have been lying about the number of times he'd looked at porn? Yes. But we encourage people to believe the truth will come out. If a spouse is lying, reality will surface sooner or later.

When we overreact to our spouse's sin, we're shooting ourselves in the foot. We may think we're causing pain in the other person, but we're just hurting ourselves by making matters worse. In fact, overreaction to our spouse's sin can be just as damaging to a marriage as the sin itself! We need to seek understanding before we form conclusions or make decisions.

That involves "leaning in," too. When we remain open to a spouse's viewpoint, we're leaning in toward our spouse. This sends the message that our spouse is important and that we're humble enough to hear his or her side of the issue.

No human is perfect; we need to allow our spouse to mess up. If we crucify our mate for hurting us, we send the message that we think he or she is worthless and unimportant. That sets up the marriage for a crisis.

Certainly some actions are unacceptable. Abuse, for instance, is not okay in any marriage. But before we jump out of a marriage, we'd better get help to ensure that we're making the right choice.

The young wife in our story was ready to throw it all away. Thankfully, she did come and see us and was willing to listen and change her response.

forgiveness

If you've been hurt by your spouse's mistake, you need to forgive. The Bible is crystal clear on this. Jesus even goes so far as to say that God won't forgive us if we don't forgive others (Matthew 6:14-15).

Like most things in life, forgiveness is a process. It starts with a choice. This is part of taking responsibility in a marriage. Often we can't do it alone, though; we need to tap into God's power. Sometimes forgiveness can feel impossible, and that's when we need to go to God in prayer. If you've formed a PIT Crew (see Chapter 6), it can help you with forgiveness, too.

> **When something negative happens and you don't know what to do, lean in.**

Forgiveness is not about accepting the wrong behavior; it's about releasing that person from your retribution. Here's an exercise that might help you find a sense of closure concerning the offense against you.

In a room by yourself, place two chairs facing each other. Sit in one chair and "talk" to your spouse as if he or she is in the other chair. You can pretend you're an attorney, presenting your stack of evidence against him or her. You can cry, yell, blame, shame, and criticize.

Then serve as that person's judge: "I find you guilty of all charges."

Finally, still in the judge's role, "release the prisoners"—both yourself and the offender.

You can release your spouse and still draw boundaries of protection. When you release someone, you aren't in bondage to anger and hurt anymore, and you don't expect that person to change. By not expecting your mate to change, you give him or her *room* to grow and change. It sounds like a paradox, but we've seen it happen over and over.

It's okay to have a wall of protection. But *lean into* the wall and peek over it without expectation or bitterness to see whether the other person might be growing after all.

when you're the offender

Now you know how to lean in if you're at the receiving end of your spouse's sin. But what if you're the cause of your spouse's hurt?

You can lean in when you've hurt your spouse by . . .

- allowing your spouse to feel whatever he or she is feeling.
- letting your spouse have a different opinion.
- being patient.

Allowing your spouse to feel bad seems counterintuitive. Feeling guilty for hurting your spouse, you may want the pain to end as quickly as possible—not just for your spouse's sake, but for yours as well. But this doesn't work if you want your marriage to be happy; it short-circuits the process.

Negative feelings aren't necessarily bad. They just *are*. Strange as it may sound, giving your spouse the right and opportunity to hurt is a gift.

We aren't encouraging you to "rub in" the hurt you've caused. We're asking you not to rush the process of healing and forgiveness your spouse needs to go through. The more you push your spouse to move on, the more he or she will resist.

The second way to lean in when you've hurt your spouse is to allow for a difference of opinion. Maybe you feel what you did wasn't such a big deal. But if your spouse feels it is, then it is.

We told that young man whose wife found the porn not to minimize her opinion. He felt strongly that she was overreacting and being unfair. But the problem in arguing with your spouse's opinion is that it usually gets stronger after you've argued about it.

This young husband had to allow his wife to feel that watching porn was equal to (or even worse than) having an affair. Did we agree with her? Not really, but we had to acknowledge that she felt that way.

> **When we overreact to our spouse's sin, we're shooting ourselves in the foot.**

The more we try to invalidate our spouse's reality, the worse the conflict is going to get. Respect your spouse's differences and watch how the confrontation begins to calm down.

If you've hurt your spouse, you can also lean in by being patient. There's no rush when it comes to the healing process. In some cases time helps; in other cases, people help more.

The worst thing we can do is rush the mending. It sends a message to our spouse that we think his or her emotions and needs are ridiculous and unfounded. These aren't things we want our spouse to feel—unless we want an unhappy marriage.

the retaliation game

When you're the offending party, one of the best ways to shoot yourself in the foot is to have one of the following attitudes:
- *The heck with it.*
- *If he (or she) believes I'm a bad person, then I might as well be one.*
- *I know this will hurt him (or her), so I'll do it.*

This retaliation game doesn't work! You just end up hurting yourself and spiraling the relationship downward.

At one of our intensives a couple was having a difficult time with finances. The wife was upset because checks kept bouncing. She was in the habit of belittling her husband, with the result that he felt like a failure. His self-defeating reaction was to withdraw money from an ATM to get gas, then file the gas receipt in his truck for reimbursement from his company—but wad up and throw away the ATM receipt he knew his wife needed. That's why the checks were bouncing.

I (Amy) said to him, "You realize you are shooting yourself in the foot, right?"

"Yes," he replied. The desire to retaliate against his wife was too great. He wanted to hurt her for demeaning him, but in the long run it just hurt him because he lost money with the overdraft fees.

We hope you don't make the same mistake. Use the power of one to bring your spouse closer—not to drive him or her further away.

the right direction

Why do we lean in? Because it's far better than leaning away! Much of marriage is about feeling connected and loved. How can we feel these things if we're leaning away from each other by being judgmental, argumentative, invalidating, and impatient?

Leaning in helps our spouse to succeed in being healthy. When we lean in we create an environment that feels safe—safe for sharing feelings and needs and not worrying about getting punished for it. Leaning in also allows us to humble ourselves; who doesn't want to be around someone who's humble? Jesus washed the feet of the disciples because He humbly loved them. We express that kind of humility when we lean in.

Leaning in keeps us engaged in the marriage instead of pulling away. We can encourage all sorts of havoc in our spouse if we withdraw;

designed as we are for relationships, we can feel it when someone disengages from us. It's a horrible sensation, and can lead to feeling insecure. Insecurity can lead to a host of problems in the marriage, not the least of which is jealousy. When jealousy creeps into a marriage, watch out! Things tend to get progressively worse very quickly. Jealousy is a happiness killer because it reeks of selfishness and fear.

Finally, leaning in keeps your marriage headed in the right direction. Marriages get lost because they have no direction or they're headed the wrong way. Leaning in keeps us focused on what's right and good for our relationship.

So what happened to the young couple we talked about at the beginning of this chapter? We received a call from them not long ago. They reported being "shocked" by how much they'd grown since our intensive with them!

They were shocked because they didn't believe their trial could produce anything but pain. If you belong to Christ, you don't need to fear trouble. God uses it to increase our love for Him and for each other (James 1:2-4).

This doesn't mean we'll never hurt or have painful memories; those are a part of life. But when we lean into God and into our spouse, we can experience great healing.

it's never about the facts

"Just the facts, ma'am."

These famous words were uttered by Jack Webb, playing Sergeant Joe Friday, on the classic television series *Dragnet*.

Ever since, unhappy spouses have taken the same approach with each other—whether they realized it or not.

If you want a happy marriage, part of the surprising solution is to get off the facts and onto what really matters in the conflict. This takes a lot of personal maturity; it's much easier to argue with your spouse about details than it is to listen and try to understand his or her point of view.

consider the source

When you focus on facts during a conflict, you'll experience a negative relationship. Things won't feel good in your marriage as long as you stay stuck on the details. It's not about the facts, and most "facts" in marital battles are really a matter of opinion or perspective anyway.

Unhappy couples tend to argue about the facts surrounding conflict instead of dealing with the *source* of the conflict. Concentrating on facts is like believing the tip is all there is to an iceberg. There's so much more to a conflict than when and where it happened, who was there, what you wore, or the size of the ozone layer at the time! Conflict never erupts over facts alone, yet couples the world over want to focus on the facts.

This focus creates disharmony in your marriage as you become

like opposing attorneys during a trial. How often do you see opposing attorneys hug and kiss after a long battle in court? Never! No marriage is going to experience the joy of intimacy when conflict is
handled as if it were a lawsuit.

We can't take on the mentality of legal counsel when we get into
conflict because it forces us to avoid the root cause. If we're battling
to prove ourselves right, we miss an opportunity to understand what
truly causes our conflict. If we don't understand why we're arguing,
coming to a healthy understanding is fairly impossible.

meek, not weak

Acting like lawyers also taps into our pride. As Proverbs 11:2 (NIV)
says, "When pride comes, then comes disgrace, but with humility
comes wisdom."

If pride leads to disgrace, how does disgrace affect a marriage? It
tears down trust and the ability to see the relationship realistically.
When someone feels disgraced, any emotion is amplified. If you were
feeling upset before getting disgraced, then afterward you're going to
be livid.

Humility, on the other hand, brings wisdom—because humble
people are willing to listen. Pride closes the ears, but humility opens
them up to receive influence and understanding.

Psalm 37:11 (NIV) says, "But the meek will inherit the land and
enjoy great peace." Peace and understanding are at the heart of happy
marriages; no one gets married in order to battle a spouse every day.
Yet years of conflict and pride can create a marriage in which two people don't want to stay together.

We recently ran across a sermon by Grady Scott, pastor of Grace
Temple Missionary Baptist Church in Tucson, Arizona, titled "Blessed
are the Meek." He defines meekness as "strength under control."[1]
The Greek word for meek, he explains, is used to describe a soothing
medicine, a gentle breeze, or a broken colt. Meekness is not weakness.

If you want a happier marriage, you need to keep your emotions under control. Allow yourself the chance to be meek. The more control you have over your reactions, the stronger and more stable you'll feel. An attitude of meekness not only helps your marriage, but your relationship with God. As Psalm 138:6 (NIV) puts it, "Though the LORD is on high, he looks upon the lowly, but the proud he knows from afar."

When we stick to arguing facts, we stick with an attitude of pride. This not only disconnects us from each other, it distances us from God. When that happens, what help is there for our marriage?

further than facts

Many people truly believe that if they could just convince their spouse of the "truth," their conflict would end. The problem is that the conflict never ends when we stick to the facts. It forces us to take sides. It's an endless cycle because facts can always be argued against.

Part of the surprising solution is to get off the facts and onto what really matters in the conflict.

You have your opinion; your spouse has his or hers. Stay on facts and you'll go round and round 'til the cows come home.

When you stick to the facts, you communicate only on a surface level. Imagine a big "V," with feelings and intimacy at the bottom; disconnection and facts are at the top. If you want to get to intimacy, you have to share feelings and not just facts.

Sometimes spouses don't feel comfortable or safe sharing their feelings. They want to stay on the fact level because, frankly, they don't want connection and intimacy. Maybe you've been hurt in the past when you shared your feelings, and so you avoid sharing because it makes you too vulnerable. But you can't avoid the way you were created. God made you with the desire to connect and be intimate; you just need to find a way to share feelings in a way that can be received and honored.

Conflict is seldom about the truth. (If you're a left-brained thinker, you might be angry with us at the moment, but allow us to explain.) That's because marital fact-finding usually isn't about truth-finding; it's often a hostile effort to prove each other wrong.

In Ephesians 4:1-3 (NIV) Paul tells the church in Ephesus how to be unified in the body of Christ. "As a prisoner for the Lord, then, I urge you to live a life worthy of the calling you have received. Be completely humble and gentle; be patient, bearing with one another in love. Make every effort to keep the unity of the Spirit through the bond of peace." Later, in verse 15, Paul urges "speaking the truth in love."

I (Amy) often question myself when I speak the truth and it's not gentle or loving. Was I really being truthful? If I'm only trying to prove myself right, the Bible challenges my motivation and attitude. If I can't speak the truth in love, my speech is a distortion of truth and falls into the category of "cunning and craftiness of men in their deceitful scheming" (Ephesians 4:14, NIV).

don't push the button

My (Amy's) personality leads me to see details and facts more readily than Michael's does. It's the way God made me—and I'm sure glad He did, because our house, car, and children would be neglected in many key areas if He hadn't.

My "need-to-grow" area is on display when I focus too much on details and not enough on feelings in my relationships. For example, my children need to feel *loved* more than *cleaned*. I laugh because I'm picturing me wiping chocolate off my 11-year-old daughter while she's trying to tell me something traumatic that happened at school. She may have something on her mouth that needs to be removed, but connection happens only when I honor her feelings more than my need to erase that smudge of chocolate that's driving me crazy.

Maybe you're that way, too. Or perhaps you're the opposite, with your personality making it more difficult to choose facts over feelings. Either way, "as iron sharpens iron" (Proverbs 27:17, NIV), we're to round off each other's rough edges.

If you feel stuck in a cycle of "fact-finding" with your spouse, ask yourself these three questions:

1. Which of my "buttons" is getting pushed in this situation? Failure, control, disconnection, rejection, devaluing?

2. How am I feeling in our marriage? Like a failure, controlled, disconnected, rejected, devalued?

3. Am I helping our marriage or hurting it right now?

If we keep coming back to your "buttons," we're doing it on purpose. All conflict centers around your buttons getting pushed. You feel upset because you feel disconnected, rejected, controlled, or like a failure. The more quickly you identify your button, the more quickly you can begin discussing what's really bothering you.

> **All conflict centers around your buttons getting pushed.**

When you ask, "How am I feeling in our marriage?" you're asking yourself to be honest about the moment. For instance, are you getting stuck on facts because you're wiped out? Knowing the answer to this question helps you evaluate how you're interpreting the conflict. If you're tired, you're going to feel more sensitive than usual.

Take stock of your level of happiness; maybe you're not seeing things accurately. When you feel bankrupt inside, for example, you feel things more intensely. Once you identify where you are emotionally in your marriage, you can adjust your thinking accordingly. You can tell yourself, *Maybe I'm not being realistic.* This increases your chance of connecting with your spouse and being understood.

Since this is a book about personal responsibility, the third and final question is especially important: "Am I helping our marriage or hurting it right now?"

That query gives you the chance to be humble. If you're feeling stuck in your marriage, maybe you have more to do with your dilemma than you thought. We're rarely innocent; there's always something to hang our sinful hat on when it comes to marital conflict. We need to say to ourselves, *I'm not perfect. So what might I be doing that's making things worse right now?*

helping your marriage feel better

Remember the movie *Patch Adams?* Starring Robin Williams, it was based on the true story of Hunter "Patch" Adams, an unconventional doctor. When Patch was a patient in a psychiatric ward, his roommate had a delusional fear of squirrels—making it impossible for the roommate to go to the restroom because the squirrels might attack him.

Patch came up with a brilliant idea: Pretend to shoot the squirrels with an imaginary gun so that the roommate could "safely" go to the bathroom.

The fact was that there were no evil squirrels. But instead of sticking with this fact, Patch supported his friend. Patch kept his own reality but honored his friend enough to go to battle on his behalf. After that, the roommate had fewer and fewer irrational episodes.

When we feel the support of people we trust, we have the energy to challenge our fears and our assumptions about what's real. It's not about changing our own perception of reality; it's about understanding the other person's reality and honoring it, thereby setting him or her up to consider a different way of thinking.

The more you work on getting off the facts and onto your feelings, the better your marriage is going to feel. Focusing on facts sucks the good vibes right out of your relationship. When you get off the facts and onto what truly matters to both of you, you give the marriage a chance at experiencing joy.

Fewer facts equal more joy and happiness. Isn't that what you signed on for when you got married?

9

why your spouse
is always right

What happens when two babies of the family get married? Nothing.

And that's the problem.

Two babies wait for each other to make something happen, just as we did growing up. Babies of the family learn fairly quickly that other people will take care of them and do the dirty work. So when we got married, both being babies, we waited for each other to take care of things.

This is generally not a good plan for adults. But it's what we knew.

Sometimes, however, this can come up and bite us on the bottoms! Take the time we were closing on a house—and forgot about it until the last minute. We'd been trying to sell this house for nearly four stinking months, with over 100 showings! It was a living, breathing nightmare. You'd think our desire to sell would have helped us remember the closing date, but it didn't.

The morning of our closing came. But I (Michael) had booked a Marriage Restoration Intensive with a couple. In our intensives we lock ourselves away with the couple for eight straight hours; the closing was at 2 P.M., and we hadn't discussed how we were going to manage both events. Where were our older siblings when we needed them?

Our dilemma dawned on Amy at about 8:30 A.M. She called me, panicked about how I was going to get to the closing and not neglect the couple I was supposed to see. Explaining a plan she'd already devised, she went into great detail about what I needed to do, when I needed to do it, and how I was going to do it. She outlined how I would break for lunch at 1:45 P.M. so I could rush to the closing down the street. She'd get me lunch from Sonic Drive-In; I'd sign the documents and then head back to the intensive.

I felt controlled, to put it mildly.

I almost reacted over the phone. But then I remembered what we teach couples: "Don't rush to judgment." Every once in a while I feel obligated to actually *try* some of the things we tell others to do!

So I asked a question. I responded—quite politely if I say so myself— "Hey, this is feeling kind of controlling to me. Are you meaning for me not to have a choice in this matter?"

I waited for her to confirm my negative beliefs. But she threw a curve ball. "Oh, I'm so sorry. I did not mean to come across controlling. What are your ideas?"

Snap! I was wrong! She wasn't trying to control me—and to make matters worse, she asked for my opinion.

I was ill-prepared to share my ideas. All I'd thought about so far was how I was going to slam her for being controlling. I needed to come up with a plan, and quick.

"Well," I said finally, "I've put a lot of thought into this. And I think that instead of leaving at 1:45 P.M., I need to leave at 1:44 P.M. And I don't want to eat my Sonic immediately; I'd rather wait 'til after I sign the documents."

Amy mocked me, of course, because I didn't have a better plan. But at least I had input. Good or bad, it was input.

the value of validation

Perhaps you can relate to that story. One of you does something that gets taken in the wrong way, and the two of you start a nasty fight. We've done it, and you probably have, too.

What prevented us from getting into a massive conflict that morning? Michael's question was a good move. Asking questions helps calm the situation immediately, but you already know that.

Something else happened, and it's the focus of this chapter. I (Amy) *validated* Michael's feeling of being controlled. Instead of reacting negatively to his question, I simply received his feelings and accepted them. I acknowledged how Michael reacted to my phone call and my plan.

Validation is one of my favorite subjects. It was one of the core con-

> *You don't need your mate to validate you first, even though it feels good.*

cepts that helped Michael and me pull out of our early marriage crisis. We were headed for divorce within our first six months because we were doing a horrible job of validating each other.

Validation is a surprisingly simple solution because anyone can do it—independent of his or her spouse! You don't need your mate to validate you first, even though it feels good. You can take the initiative to validate your spouse in a conflict. When you do, you affect the marriage immediately.

One of our biggest desires in a conflict is simply to be validated. Taking the initiative to validate your spouse quickly allows you to improve the relationship and set up an environment in which you both can experience true happiness.

Let's define what we mean by validation. This can be one of those scary, confusing relationship words. Validation is showing that your spouse (or someone else) is more important to you than proving yourself right. To validate someone's feelings is first to accept those feelings and then acknowledge and accept the other person's unique identity and individuality.

Validation sounds like this:

"I understand how you could feel that way."

"Wow, I had no idea that my words came across like that."

There are no "buts" or "howevers" in validating. When you say something like, "Okay, I understand what you're saying, but . . ." you might as well tell your spouse to take his or her feelings and go fly a kite.

When validating, you allow people to feel how they want to feel. Whatever they *feel* is important to them can actually *be* important to them. You're respecting your spouse for his or her uniqueness and value.

Validation gives people space to change their own feelings. Those who validate well are not in the business of trying to change others' feelings or needs. They don't respond to their spouse by saying, "Well, that is ridiculous," or "I can't believe you're taking it that way!"

Validation works because you put your feelings aside and focus on honoring your spouse. James 1:19 (NIV) teaches us to slow down and listen: "My dear brothers, take note of this: Everyone should be quick to listen, slow to speak and slow to become angry." This is a powerful way to validate your spouse. When we take time to shut our mouths and listen, we send the message that our mate is valuable and worth listening to.

validation is vital

Validation is an important part of our responsibility for setting up a marriage to succeed. It's a powerful tool we can use regardless of our spouse's attitude because it has a naturally calming effect.

If you've done something to hurt or offend your spouse, and you invalidate his or her feelings by arguing, justifying, getting stuck on facts, or demeaning, the hurt he or she was feeling already has now officially and dramatically increased.

For example, let's say that on a scale from 1 to 10 (1 being no big deal and 10 being extremely big) your spouse comes to you at a 5 about something you did. If you choose to invalidate his or her feelings or needs, that 5 just became a 7 or 8. When people get their feelings invalidated, they don't naturally calm down. They get even more upset! Invalidating your spouse only makes whatever was going on worse.

The good news is that the opposite is true if you choose to validate your spouse. If she comes to you at a 5 and you validate her, suddenly her 5 shrinks to a 2 or 3. When I validated Michael on the day of our closing, he went from a 7 or 8 to a 3 or 4. I could hear him step away from his negative beliefs and backtrack from his critical spirit.

Why is validation critical to a happy marriage? Because when our spouse is upset, the main thing he or she wants is for his or her feelings and needs to be heard and respected.

> *Validating your spouse is a choice, not a natural response to conflict.*

Conflict resolution can't begin until we validate those feelings and needs.

The first thing we do in our Marriage Restoration Intensive program is teach couples how to validate each other. This sets the tone for the entire day. Both partners tend to relax a little more after they've been validated. Usually they're experiencing being validated for the first time in a long time; couples in crisis tend to be very poor at validating each other because they're wiped out emotionally.

We want to be honest: Validation is an extremely mature thing to do. The more self-centered you are, the more difficult it will be to validate. This is why it has so much to do with personal responsibility. Validating your spouse is a choice, not a natural response to conflict.

the verbs of validation

Validating doesn't have to feel impossible or unrealistic. You *can* do this; you just have to *want* to. A happy marriage is possible, but only if you're willing to work at it.

And here's what you'll be working at:
- acknowledging your spouse's feelings
- identifying the feelings by asking specific questions or echoing specific statements
- offering to listen, which means stopping any other activity and leaning toward your spouse
- helping your spouse clearly define his or her feelings by rewording what you hear
- being there for your spouse spiritually, physically, and emotionally
- being patient when your spouse is sharing
- trying not to rush him or her through the experience of sharing
- accepting your spouse's feelings and needs without being judgmental

The last part probably is the most important, and often is the most difficult. Accepting our spouse's feelings or needs without judging is hard to do, especially if we feel our spouse is being unfair or misunderstanding us.

Early in our marriage, Amy struggled with my sarcasm. She did not find sarcasm funny—at all. She took it as cruelty, meanness, and downright ugliness toward her. I wasn't trying to be any of those things; in my heart, I was truly attempting to bond and connect with her. As I've told Gary Chapman (author of the best-selling *The Five Love Languages*), there needs to be a sixth love language: sarcasm. It's the Smalley way of connecting.

We went round and round over this issue. Amy would react negatively to my sarcasm by saying something like, "You are so mean!"

I would respond with equal intensity by saying something like, "No I'm not!"

Then the cycle would escalate:

AMY: Yes, you are!

MICHAEL: No, I'm not!

AMY: Yes . . . you are!

MICHAEL: No . . . I'm not!

It wasn't until we learned to validate each other that this conflict was resolved. The solution was easy; I needed to acknowledge Amy's feelings of hurt over my sarcasm. When I asked her what I needed to do to make it right, she told me to please stop being sarcastic with her. So I did.

Accepting your spouse's feelings or needs without judging is hard to do.

When validation happens, negative feelings tend to dissipate. The combatants calm down. This incident was a perfect example.

It's also an example of how things can change when one person takes action. For months after that I avoided sarcasm with Amy. Then one day she took the opportunity to slam *me* over something I'd done. It was a really funny slam, though. If I hadn't validated her first, she probably never would have gotten to a place where she felt comfortable joking like that with me.

Today Amy and I have fun with sarcasm. But we wouldn't be able to do that unless I'd validated her feelings and needs.

roadblocks to validation

Are there certain attitudes that keep you from validating your spouse? Take a look at the following roadblocks and think about how they may have affected your marriage.

1. *Not wanting to admit you made a mistake.* Validation doesn't mean you're admitting to being wrong or a jerk. Remember, validation is not primarily about right, wrong, or even truth. It means you see how the other person could have interpreted your actions or words in a particular way.

2. *Not wanting your spouse to take advantage of you.* "If I validate him, he'll think it's fine to keep doing whatever he wants." Instead of

making a negative assumption about your spouse, use open-ended questions to find out what he or she is thinking.

3. *Resentment or unresolved anger.* Sometimes we don't want to validate because of unresolved anger that's turned to bitterness. Anger in itself is not wrong, but the Bible warns against sinning as a result of our anger (Ephesians 4:26).

4. *Pride.* "Why should I have to validate?" It's a question we hear all the time from couples in crisis. "Why can't I just be me?" The answer: Because being ourselves usually means being messed up!

5. *Guilt.* "If I validate her feelings, I was wrong; that means I'm a bad person." We all cause hurt; no one is free from sin. If you did the wrong thing, ask forgiveness. Take responsibility. Fully embracing your role results in fully embracing your relationship.

the validity of validation

So why do you need to validate?

Because when your spouse feels validated, the energy to fight gets sucked out of the relationship. It's like pouring a huge bucket of water on a fire. The passion or need to fight gets lost and you begin to connect with each other again.

Validation is a huge way for you to bring your marriage together—whether or not your mate does the same.

taking time-outs

What you're about to learn is vital to encouraging and maintaining a happy marriage. If you can't do this one thing, then all the other stuff in this book is going to be useless.

Remember our central message: You have the power to make a change in your marriage, even if your spouse is not trying or is even doing the wrong thing. But what if conflict erupts? How can the "power of one" influence two people who are poised for battle?

Calming down during conflict is an incredibly powerful tool for keeping conflict on a healthy level. If you want your marriage to be happier, you need to learn how to defuse bombs instead of arming them.

We can't emphasize enough how important it is to learn how to call a time-out—even if it's only for yourself. Time-outs are your key defense against hurtful and meaningless conflict, and against letting a confrontation spiral out of control.

conflicts of interest

Why does conflict hurt so many marriages? Because so many couples never learn how to handle it appropriately.

And because most couples get into conflict when their ability to think clearly is gone.

Drs. Howard Markman and Scott Stanley at the University of Denver have been researching couples for 25 years. They discovered during one study[1] that when a male's heart rate gets above 90 beats per minute, his ability to think and talk rationally goes out the window. The researchers also found that if they simply interrupted a conflict by asking a couple to read a newspaper for 5-10 minutes, the spouses calmed down enough to have a relatively healthy discussion about the conflict. So time-outs help resolve conflicts and keep hurt feelings to a minimum.

Time-outs are your key defense against hurtful and meaning-less conflict.

They also help to prevent meaningless conflict. You know that kind. It's the type that, when the feelings finally calm down, makes you look back and think, *What in the world were we just fighting about?*

Meaningless conflict tends to happen when you've simply had a bad day and overreact to something your spouse did innocently (or not so innocently). A time-out helps eliminate this kind of conflict because you never really get going. And once the time-out is over, you realize the disagreement wasn't important enough to keep discussing. Your tension is relaxed, and whatever it was you were upset about is over.

avoiders and escalators

So what is a time-out? First of all, you need to know it's not the same as *avoiding* a conflict.

Often there are two kinds of "conflict personalities" in a marriage: one who *avoids* conflict at all costs and one who *engages* in conflict at all costs. These are *avoiders* and *escalators*, two terms which also come from the research of Drs. Markman and Stanley. Both personalities can be destructive to a marriage because neither helps conflict get resolved.

Avoiders can hurt a relationship because they never actually engage in a discussion; they try to bury their hurt feelings or anger deep down inside. Of course, you never bury anger dead; you always bury it alive. So at some point it's going to build beyond the avoider's ability to contain it, and will explode like a volcano. In our intensives, we usually can identify avoiders by the statements of their spouse: "I had no idea my husband was so angry! It was like this came out of the blue!"

It can be hard to identify avoiders because they present such a calm appearance and try to convince you that nothing is wrong. But something *is* wrong. Trouble comes to the marriage because the non-avoiding spouse has no idea something is amiss.

Escalators are much easier to spot. They put their thoughts, feelings, and opinions out there for all the world to see. Rarely is there any confusion surrounding the thoughts and feelings of an escalator. Escalators erupt right alongside the conflict, tending to yell and scream to make their points. This is destructive because they usually say or do things they don't really mean. Once something is out there, though, it's too late to take it back.

Whether you're an escalator or an avoider, you need to know how to take a time-out when negative feelings come as a result of your spouse's actions or words.

Can you tell when you're having a negative reaction? Probably. The problem may lie in the way you respond. If it involves avoiding or escalating, you're hurting the marriage. If that's the case, calling a time-out may be the greatest gift you ever give your spouse. A time-out says, "I love you and want to resolve this issue, but I can't do it right at the moment. Just give me an hour and we will come back and resolve this."

A time-out is a living, breathing example of grace. If you belong to Christ, you know that He shows an infinite amount of grace toward us. Why not show some of that grace to your spouse?

making time-outs work

To let your spouse know that you need a time-out, you might say something like the following:

- "I need a break."
- "I'm about to say something I don't mean."
- "I don't feel like this is going to a good place."
- "I'm about to lose control and do something I'm going to regret, so please allow me to take a time-out so I can calm down."

Remember to set a deadline for a time-in. Don't say to your spouse, "I can't talk about this right now," and then leave without assuring him or her when you *will* talk about it. You might want to say something like, "I think I'll be ready to talk in about two hours; is this okay with you?"

It's fine to negotiate a time to come back. Just remember to relax and be open to serving your mate's needs. If you get stubborn about how much time you want for the time-out, things are probably going to get ugly. Work out a time that's agreeable to both of you.

Now you're ready to take a break and leave each other alone. Respect each other's space during the time-out. That should help you eliminate the kind of farce that happens when you chase each other throughout the house. Demanding that your spouse talk is a bad strategy; give each other the respect you both deserve and maintain a distance during your time-out.

During the break, make sure you think about your part in the conflict. No one is 100 percent innocent; even if you can rationalize that you're responsible for only 5 percent, take 100 percent responsibility for that 5 percent.

A time-out isn't the same as avoiding a conflict.

The time-out is not an opportunity to become more upset about your spouse. Don't spend your time-out building a case against him or her. As we've said before, you're not on opposing counsel—you're on the same team. Taking a time-out to develop your argument will only make the conflict worse. If your objective is a happy marriage, you'll spend your time-out in a way that honors your spouse.

During your time apart, think about how you could have handled the situation differently. I (Amy) always think about my approach. Did I escalate or say something that was unfair or mean? Even my tone of voice can get me in trouble at times. How may I have handled myself poorly during the confrontation?

time-out for prayer

In Luke 6:28 Jesus teaches us to pray for our enemies. When you and your spouse are in conflict, you're acting like enemies. So, during your time-out, take time to pray.

Go to God honestly. He already knows your heart anyway, so trying to hide negative feelings is kind of like standing in the middle of Central Park and believing no one can see you. God already knows what you're thinking, so let it all out.

If you have trouble being honest with God, ask: *What am I afraid of?*

Are you afraid He won't like you anymore? Do you think He will punish you for being honest? God's grace and mercy are never ending. We don't deserve them, yet He still gives them to us!

Do you fear God will act on your negative thoughts about your spouse? If you go to God moaning about how horrible your spouse is, He's not going to respond with, "I hear you, child. I can't believe you have to live with such a loser, either. I'm God, and I couldn't live with him! So what do you want from Me, My child? Do you want Me to 'take care' of this little problem of yours? I could take him out in an instant, and even make it look like an accident. I'm God; I can do anything!"

No, God is not going to answer like a cosmic Mafia boss. Instead, as He listens to you, He may begin to help you understand something you did wrong in the conflict—something for which you can take responsibility and take action to undo.

The power of prayer is in opening yourself up to listen to God. Before you know it, you may be asking God to forgive you for your part in the conflict. That's a humbling experience.

time for time-in

Before the time-out is over, ask yourself if you're ready to validate your spouse's feelings. If you aren't, reschedule another meeting time. A good rule of thumb is that the person who calls the time-out is the one who calls the time-in. It's okay to remind your spouse if needed; you could say something like, "Hey, I thought we were going to talk in two hours. Is that still alright?"

During your time apart, think about how you could have handled the situation differently.

A humble spirit is necessary for a healthy discussion. You can't find solutions until you're willing to hear both sides.

Once you're ready to listen, you're ready to talk. When you can validate your spouse, you're ready to talk. When you try to have God's perspective, you're ready to talk. Don't attempt to talk until you're humble and prepared to acknowledge your part in the conflict.

The power of a time-out is that it humbles and prepares you. Those are the very things you'll need to resolve the conflict—whether or not your spouse is similarly equipped.

correcting and connecting

Have you ever jumped off an emotional cliff because you were convinced your spouse was guilty of something? You had such a negative belief about your spouse's action or intent that you convinced yourself you were right and your spouse was the crazy one. You were so sure of your belief that not even actual evidence to the contrary could persuade you of your possible error in judgment!

You're not alone.

This chapter is about being fair with your spouse. By "fair" we mean that you need to eliminate or at least check out your negative beliefs about your spouse. If you believe your spouse doesn't like your parents, for instance, this chapter will help you take responsibility for that belief and check it out in a loving, productive way. Most of the time, your negative beliefs will be exposed as groundless—if you have the courage to check them out.

the mind-reading myth

Couples come to our intensive program with runaway negative beliefs about each other. But one time, I (Michael) met a wife who put the rest to shame. She believed so profoundly that her husband didn't like her that it was destroying their marriage.

I started by encouraging the wife to describe what a fun date night would be for her. I like couples to start off discussing mundane or safe issues. Typically, having a couple describe a great date night is a safe way to begin. In this case, I couldn't have been more wrong!

It started off fairly well. The husband did a good job repeating her feelings and needs. Then it was the husband's turn to share what a fun date night would be for him.

This was when the conversation got funky.

The husband said going out to dinner and a movie would be fun for him. Looking to the wife, encouraging her to repeat what the husband said, I noticed tears forming in her eyes.

What did she hear her husband say? I thought. For the life of me, I couldn't imagine what might have been offensive or hurtful in what the husband shared. His attitude was positive and his words were fair and kind.

I figured I would let the wife respond, then ask her what the tears were about. But she beat me to the punch.

As she began to repeat her husband's words, the negative beliefs came screaming to the surface. "What I heard you say," she sobbed as the tears literally streamed down her face, "was that you want to go out to eat because you hate my cooking. . . . You've always hated my cooking, and I'll never be as good as your mother!"

> **You need to eliminate or at least check out your negative beliefs about your spouse.**

The husband gave me a questioning glance, looking for some assurance or guidance. Unfortunately, I had the same look on my face.

I knew what was wrong; I just had never seen it so blatantly before. This wife had a profound belief that her husband hated her cooking—and probably hated her as well.

As this wife would discover, her belief about her husband was way off. After helping her calm down, I had her ask a clarifying question: "Do you hate my cooking, and is that why you want to go out for dinner on our date nights?"

This was a hard question for her to ask, but an important one.

She was sure her husband's answer would be, "Yes, I hate you *and* your cooking, and I wish you would just leave me forever!"

But her husband's response was incredible! It was a classic example of why we need to ask clarifying questions.

With tears now running down *his* cheeks, the husband replied, "Honey, I love your cooking. You're the best cook I've ever known! The reason I want us to go out to dinner is because you are the one always stuck in the kitchen serving everyone in the family. I want to eat out to give you a break so *you* can be served for once."

Wow! She couldn't have been more off with her beliefs! Seconds after the husband's response, they were hugging and kissing.

Would you like more hugging and kissing in your marriage? Learn how to ask clarifying questions. You'll experience a happier, more fulfilling relationship instead of running around with false, negative beliefs about your spouse.

The point of this chapter is to help you ask those questions rather than running amok with damaging assumptions. Negative beliefs wreak all kinds of havoc on marital satisfaction. Clarifying questions help eliminate negative beliefs—especially the false ones.

clear as mud?

Clarifying questions are worded specifically to investigate a negative belief. For example, if you believe your spouse hates your family, you need to find out whether that's true. You might ask something like, "For some reason I get the feeling you don't like my family. Is this accurate?"

Notice how the beginning of the statement is humble and soft. Clarifying questions can't come across as mean or judgmental. Keep your mind open to the possibility that your belief might be mistaken. Your humility softens the heart of your spouse to receive your question.

Let's pretend you believe that your spouse doesn't like going out on dates. This might not feel as intense as other potential issues, like the belief your spouse is cheating on you. But the longer a negative assumption percolates in your mind, the more time it has to get worse.

Keep your mind open to the possibility that your belief might be mistaken.

Ask your mate, "Do you like going out on dates?" You might be surprised at what you discover. Your spouse may validate your negative belief by answering affirmatively, or might add a clarification like, "It's not that I hate going out on dates with you; I would just like to try something other than dinner and a movie."

Clarifying questions give your spouse a chance to correct and connect. I (Amy) learned this early in our marriage when I was convinced that Michael disliked my family. When we first got married he was quiet, shy, and not very funny around my relatives. I tried to push him to open up and be himself, but it didn't happen. The more I pushed, the more Michael pulled away.

I would ask him often, "You don't like my family, do you?" Not exactly a gentle clarifying question, but it was honest.

He would reply, "I like your family just fine."

So I asked a softer question: "Why aren't you funny around them?"

"I don't know," he said. "I just don't know how I'm supposed to act. I don't feel comfortable around them yet."

Eventually I realized that the more I thought Michael didn't like my relatives, the more he would worry about it—and the more he wouldn't be able to be himself around them. So I dialed down the intensity of my interrogations.

That doesn't mean, though, that we should stop asking appropriate questions that could help us understand each other. When you don't ask clarifying questions, you run the risk of pushing each other to have extreme feelings and take extreme positions on circumstances and issues in the absence of real information.

Clarifying questions also can help when the meaning of a statement isn't clear. A sentence can be interpreted in many different ways, based on the stress of certain words. Take this one we heard in an intensive recently: "This is the last counseling I am going to."

That can mean a lot of different things. I (Amy) asked the husband who said it, "What did you mean by what you just said? Did you mean after today you are done? Or did you mean you are tired of going from person to person for help, and so you are here today and in the future—but you don't want to keep switching counselors or marriage consultants?"

At that point he said, "It's the second thing you said. I want to get help, but I don't want to have to start all over again with a different person."

If we hadn't asked what he meant, his wife could have felt boxed in, defensive, and hopeless. She could have heard him saying, "I'm done, don't care, and I quit!"

But that would have been wrong. We gave him the opportunity to clarify his statement; it's a good idea to do the same for your spouse.

trust, but verify

When we make assumptions, we set ourselves up to expect worst-case scenarios more than anything else. Clarifying questions can be used as a buffer, or a deep breath, before jumping to the wrong conclusion. The bigger the hurt, the harder it is to be realistic about your spouse's meaning or intentions.

We know it's difficult to give someone who's hurt you the benefit of the doubt, especially if he or she has proven untrustworthy. Checking out our negative beliefs with clarifying questions is an attempt to rebuild trust.

As President Ronald Reagan said during the Cold War, "Trust, but verify." If trust has been broken, verification is a must. It's part of reconciling the relationship.

Taking the lead in asking clarifying questions can go a long way toward strengthening your marriage. Honesty is fostered when we refrain from judgment and have open-ended discussion: "I'm not blaming you. I know we had some unexpected medical bills this month, but can we sit down and talk about how our American Express bill got so high?"

By clarifying what you *don't* mean, you can help your spouse hear what you *do*.

the trillion-dollar question

One of our darkest nights took place only six months into our marriage.

In those early days we didn't understand how to resolve conflict, and it almost led to our marital demise. We also stank at *repairing* conflict. There's a difference between resolving and repairing. Resolving involves communication and validation; repairing involves just one question.

It's the Trillion-dollar Question—the TDQ.

Perhaps you're hurting in your marriage. Maybe you feel stuck on some continual conflict with your spouse. When you take the initiative to ask the Trillion-dollar Question, you begin the process of restoring your marriage and getting unstuck.

This question is a result of your choice to move forward by embracing your spouse's feelings and needs. You might not want to ask the question because you're hurting; but you're hurting *because you probably have not asked this question.*

jump-starting your marriage

What almost destroyed us that dark night only six months into our marriage? Thinking back on it, we both agree it had a lot to do with our immaturity and lack of premarital education. In those days we fought about everything—from remembering wallets to remembering to be somewhere on time.

The worst part was how poor we were at repairing the conflict.

Neither of us was asking the Trillion-dollar Question, which is why we make it such a major part of our work with couples today.

I (Michael) vividly remember running out of the log cabin we were living in. It was about 2 A.M., and there was no moon to light my way through the night. I ran and ran until I tired out and plopped on the ground—which, sadly, only took a couple hundred yards. (Okay, maybe it was more like 75 yards, but it felt like a million miles at the time!)

Learning how to ask the Trillion-dollar Question is like giving a massive jump-start to your relationship.

Lying in the middle of the road, I thought about how much I wanted a truck to come by and run over me. I was that miserable! Since it was the middle of the night on a private road in the middle of nowhere, the chance of a truck coming by at that hour was pretty much zero. But I was hurting and wanted the pain to end.

If you want a happier marriage than we had at that point, you need to learn how to ask your spouse what it will take to make it happy. For a marriage to be truly satisfying, you need to be willing to ask how it can be better. That's a step you can take on your own if necessary.

This very evening I helped a young man in the parking lot of Target. His car was dead, so I offered to jump-start it. I was thinking about this chapter, realizing how the TDQ is very much like jolting a battery to life. Learning how to ask the Trillion-dollar Question is like giving a massive jump-start to your relationship. It gives you the energy that can get things moving in the right direction.

so what's the question?

What is this Trillion-dollar Question? It's quite simple, actually, but is rarely used by couples who are struggling. (We used to call it the

Million-dollar Question, but in today's economy a million doesn't go as far as it used to!) It takes maturity, action, decision, and brute force to ask. But it's worth it because of the relational returns. Emotional bank accounts burst at the seams when you learn to ask this question.

The question is this: "What can I do to repair with you?"

Or, to put it in plainer English, it could be any of the following:

"What can I do to make this right?"

"What do you need from me at this moment?"

"How can I help you right now?"

"Is there anything you need from me?"

All these questions lead your spouse down the road toward repairing conflict.

That's good, because if you're anything like us, you get into conflict all the time. If we've said it a thousand times at our seminars, we'll say it a thousand times more: *We are not compatible!*

One of the reasons we believe any couple can make it is because we've made it! If we can learn how to get along, anyone can. Perhaps God brought us together because He knew we'd be forced to learn how to get along, repair, and communicate because of our differences. For us, the TDQ has been an important part of that process.

the TDQ in action

We were working with a couple once who hurt from the effects of an affair. The husband and wife were separated as a result of his infidelity; the wife had asked him to move out of the house and had rejected his many attempts to apologize and repair the damage he'd caused.

It was a two-day intensive, and for half of the first day the husband kept trying to say all the right things to his wife. He told her he was wrong and that it would never happen again. But she would have none of it.

His desperate attempts to repair were beginning to interfere with making progress when a thought passed through my (Michael's) head: *He hasn't asked the TDQ yet! This whole time I've been allowing him to go on and on without ever getting him to stop and simply ask his wife what she needed, if anything, to be done to repair the hurt and damage to the marriage!*

I also realized he had been consistently ending each of his attempts to apologize with the statement, "It will never happen again."

The TDQ leads your spouse down the road toward repairing conflict.

I knew why he was saying it; he felt bad and wanted to reassure his wife. But for some reason it seemed his statement was causing the opposite effect.

"Have you ever asked your wife what she needs from you to repair the hurt she is feeling?" I asked. "I mean, truly just asked her what you need to do and then patiently waited for her response?"

He sat up higher on the couch, uncomfortable for a second. Finally he responded, "No. I don't think I have ever just asked her what I need to do."

I encouraged him to ask her.

When he did, the wife didn't scream. She didn't belittle him or even attack him. She started crying, and said, "What I've wanted from the beginning was for you to ask for my forgiveness and then give me some space to figure out what I need to do. But every time I hear you say, 'It will never happen again,' it just makes me feel like you don't think it's a big deal and just want me to hurry up and be okay with what happened."

Now it was the husband's turn to start crying. He looked at his wife and said, "I had no idea that what I was doing was actually making things worse! I was trying to make things right because I feel so disgusting for what I did to you and our family. But I do ask for your forgiveness and I want to give you the space you need."

They were ready to start moving forward.

why the TDQ works

The Trillion-dollar Question works because:
- It sends the message that you care.
- It honors your spouse's unique personality.
- It gets it right the first time.
- It eliminates confusion about what to do.
- It gives you something specific to do.

When you ask your spouse, "What do you need from me at this moment?" you're sending the message that you're interested in making things right. Your spouse can melt at these words, but too many spouses never hear them uttered.

Caring involves action. It's never enough to say, "I love you," while avoiding actually doing anything that is loving. And if you don't know what your spouse would consider to be loving, you risk doing something that is well-intentioned but meaningless to him or her.

How many times have you tried to repair damage done during conflict to find that your efforts only made things worse? This is such a common occurrence! One spouse does something wrong, feels bad, and tries to repair it without asking the TDQ. Asking the Trillion-dollar Question isn't just an option; it's absolutely necessary because the health of your marriage depends on it.

If you feel bad about something you did, then try to repair it without asking what you need to do, you'll usually do things that are meaningful to *you.* You end up missing the mark. During our first tumultuous months of marriage, I (Michael) would buy Amy flowers when trying to repair the damage after one of our fights. The problem was that because I didn't ask Amy what she wanted from me, I didn't know she hated flowers! That's right—every time I got her flowers I only ended up getting us into another fight. I'm a genius, I know!

It wasn't until we learned to start asking each other the TDQ that we actually started repairing the damage.

How does the TDQ honor your spouse's unique personality? You don't know your spouse as well as you think; the reality is that you'll never fully know him or her. The TDQ can be a big help. Sometimes people feel shallow for asking the TDQ; it's not shallow to ask, it's smart. In fact, the more you ask the TDQ, the more you get to know your spouse.

As for getting it right the first time, that's invaluable! How much time is wasted in conflict when two people are running around doing the opposite of what needs to be done? The TDQ helps cut the waste of meaningless gestures and over-budget ideas. When you ask the TDQ, you equip yourself to repair the relationship much more quickly than if you try to do it blindfolded.

God and the TDQ

Using the TDQ is a good way to buy into the central theme of this book—personal responsibility. It's also a way to live out Bible passages like Matthew 5:48: "In a word, what I'm saying is, Grow up. You're kingdom subjects. Now live like it. Live out your God-created identity. Live generously and graciously toward others, the way God lives toward you."

Jesus tells us here to treat others (including our spouse) the way He treats us! By asking this one question, we're getting closer to living the life God wants us to live.

But can you do that if you feel emotionally bankrupt? What if you're hurting and you don't seem to have the energy to ask the question?

You need to take good care of yourself if your relationships are going to succeed. Taking care of yourself is included in one of the concepts Jesus declared to the Pharisees:

When the Pharisees heard how he had bested the Sadducees, they gathered their forces for an assault. One of their religion scholars spoke for them, posing a question they hoped would show him up: "Teacher, which command in God's Law is the most important?"

Jesus said, " 'Love the Lord your God with all your passion and prayer and intelligence.' This is the most important, the first on any list. But there is a second to set alongside it: 'Love others as well as you love yourself.' These two commands are pegs; everything in God's Law and the Prophets hangs from them." (Matthew 22:34-40)

By saying, "as you love yourself," Jesus is implying that we're already doing that. It's difficult to take personal responsibility when we're bankrupt emotionally. If we're expending our energy loathing ourselves, it's going to be hard to find the strength to ask the TDQ.

Besides taking care of ourselves, we can choose to do the right thing even when we don't feel like doing it. This takes maturity. Asking the TDQ is not a feeling, it's a choice.

benefits of the TDQ

The results of the TDQ are many. For now, though, let's focus on five benefits of asking the Trillion-dollar Question.

1. *It creates an environment for happiness in your marriage.* It gets you active in making a positive difference. You're no longer on the sidelines watching your marriage; you're in the game, doing your best for the team!

2. *It creates an environment in which the two of you can feel connected.* Who doesn't feel more connected when someone asks what he or she can do to make things right? That's especially true when that someone is your spouse!

3. *It creates understanding.* You can't begin to understand your spouse until you ask questions. The TDQ helps you learn how to repair

in a way that your mate will appreciate. Even if you and your spouse are more compatible than we are, you're still different from each other.

4. *It puts the focus on the present.* The TDQ keeps the conversation about what you can do *now* instead of rehashing old disagreements. We can't change the past but we can try to clean it up. If you handled a situation poorly, the TDQ helps you find out what to do. That happened when I (Amy) misjudged someone close to me. I made an accusation that turned out to be false. After apologizing, I asked, "Is there anything else I can do?"

The person's response was amazing. She said, "It seems like if you got to know me better, you might not make the same mistake. Can we get together for coffee?"

I said, "Sure, I'd love to." The result was a closer relationship.

5. *It creates intimacy.* When you add up happiness, connection, and understanding, you get intimacy. Becoming closer is the goal of every married person on the planet. We've traveled to Africa, India, Europe, and South America, and what brings the world together is every human being's desire and need to love and feel loved. The TDQ makes that possible, and creates the environment for intimacy to thrive.

don't give up

Maybe you're wondering whether it's really worth it to ask the Trillion-dollar Question. What if you have a history of mistrust or cynicism toward your spouse? Does the TDQ work then? What if you've even been to counseling before, and it seems you always end up right back in trouble?

Don't allow the past to prevent you from doing what's healthy. The past matters, but it doesn't deserve the power to keep you from doing what's right for the relationship.

Ask the TDQ. Even if your spouse reacts negatively, that's only a sign that your relationship may need the help of a professional. Don't let your discouragement keep you from getting that help.

the power of the positive

Mark and Alicia had been married for only three months. Yet they were sitting in our office in crisis because Mark had filed for divorce.

Had there been an affair? Nope.

Had there been any abuse? Nope.

What could cause a husband to want a divorce after only three months?

Kids.

But this couple hadn't had any kids yet. Mark was filing for divorce because he wanted kids (six, to be precise) and Alicia didn't (zero, to be precise).

Their situation was unique. Surely they'd discussed their desires about children before they got married, right? Wrong! Somehow neither Mark nor Alicia had shared plans about children with the other.

Had they undergone a shotgun romance? No, they'd dated for over a year before getting married. So how did they avoid discussing children for an entire year? Their answer was, "I guess we never thought about it."

Well, they were thinking about it now.

when marriage is unhappy

What do you do when your expectations or desires for your marriage aren't met? Mark felt the only choice he had was to file for divorce.

What are *your* options? Is divorce an option for you? We hope not.

We often compare divorce to a house fire. Let's say you hate your marriage and just want the pain to end. Divorce would be as stupid as running out of a burning home, hooking a fire hose to a gas tanker,

We can't blame anyone or anything for our negative attitudes—except ourselves.

running back inside, and turning on the hose believing the gas will put the fire out! What happens when you turn on that hose? It makes the fire worse!

Divorce is not a solution to your marriage problems; it is another problem. If you feel disconnected from your spouse, imagine how disconnected you would feel after a divorce. If you think your spouse doesn't help around the house or help enough with the kids, how much more helpful will he or she be after a divorce? He or she will live a separate life in a separate home. Divorce—and you can ask anyone who's ever gotten divorced—is miserable.

Mark and Alicia's problem was not how many kids to have. It was that they believed their circumstances dictated their happiness.

Mark was stuck on the belief that he needed children to be happy. Alicia was stuck on the conviction that she needed childlessness to be happy. Neither was correct. Happiness isn't about circumstances; it's about a state of mind.

Mark and Alicia were choosing to stay focused on the negative in their relationship—as opposed to finding the positive.

what makes you happy

Depending on how you translate it, French author François de La Rochefoucauld said something like, "Happiness and misery depend as much on temperament as fortune." Happiness has more to do with your decisions and responses to circumstances than the circumstances themselves.

Issues and events do not *make* you happy or unhappy. They certainly can affect you, but they don't control your mind or your soul. Your response and attitude determine your satisfaction in life.

Jewish psychiatrist Victor Frankl, author of *Man's Search for Meaning,* discovered this very principle inside a Nazi concentration camp. Amid the horrors of that place, he found that even though the Nazis could control his food, physical condition, and living quarters, they could not control his mind or soul.

After being released from the camp, Frankl went on to establish logotherapy, a form of existential analysis used widely today. Here's how Wikipedia summarizes it:

> Frankl's concept is based on the premise that the primary motivational force of an individual is to find a meaning in life. The following list of tenets represents the basic principles of logotherapy:
> - Life has meaning under all circumstances, even the most miserable ones.
> - Our main motivation for living is our will to find meaning in life.
> - We have freedom to find meaning in what we do, and what we experience, or at least in the stand we take when faced with a situation of unchangeable suffering.[1]

How you respond to trials largely determines your level of happiness. This is important to understand; if you don't, you will live your life as a victim. We can't blame anyone or anything for our negative attitudes—except ourselves.

This chapter is about reprogramming your mind—especially if you've bought into the belief that you're not responsible for your happiness. It's opposite of the view that says, "I can't be happy because you are making me miserable!" Many of us need a radical transformation in how we perceive the challenges in our lives.

find a new mind

The first step to a stronger marriage requires ridding ourselves of negative beliefs, self-defeating attitudes, unjustified and negative explanations, and illogical conclusions. We need a new mind that doesn't offer excuses. Many assumptions from our old way of thinking must go if we're to transform our marriages.

Believing your spouse makes you unhappy is destructive and unproductive. What might happen if you focus on God and allow His grace and power to renew your mind from the inside? No more excuses, lies, or pretenses. As you begin to transform your identity from victim to hero, you'll experience the kind of change you want most in your marriage. What other choice do you have?

James 1:2 advises us to consider it pure joy when we face trouble! Why? Because trials create character and perseverance, and perseverance creates hope for our future. We're not advocating for denial here. When your spouse sins against you, it's going to hurt. Our question is, what are you going to do with that hurt? Are you going to let it sink deep down into your soul and fester, causing bitterness and unforgiveness? Or are you going to do something constructive with the hurt—like seeking the counsel of others, digging deeper into Scripture, or running as fast as you can into the arms of Jesus?

What are your biggest complaints about your marriage right now? Write them down somewhere and then read them aloud to yourself. But challenge your beliefs about them. Could you be wrong? Are they as bad as you've built them up to be? What is your part in them? The more honest you are in answering these questions, the more likely that you will redefine your complaints.

Those complaints are your biggest trials, too. What have you learned from them so far? If you're a Christian, have you experienced real growth in your relationship with Jesus as a result of any of these problems?

One of the more profound books we've read recently is by Max Lucado: *Facing Your Giants*. It pushes us to stop focusing our attention on what's wrong and broken in our lives and refocus it on God. Our favorite quote from the book is, "Focus on giants—you stumble. Focus on God—your giants tumble."

We use this quote in every Marriage Restoration Intensive we do. It's a powerful way to help couples move from crisis to happiness. But you don't have to be in crisis for this quote to help!

If you learn to live by focusing on God *before* you get in trouble, you'll be more prepared to focus on God when you *do* get in trouble. Truthfully, we wish we could learn how to keep our gaze on God all the time and not just when we're in crisis.

Proverbs 1:32-33 says, "Don't you see what happens, you simpletons, you idiots? Carelessness kills; complacency is murder. First pay at-

> **Get your focus onto what you want to happen.**

tention to me, and then relax. Now you can take it easy—you're in good hands." God is the great healer and restorer—not you, your spouse, nor other people. When you focus only on what's wrong in your marriage, you bring everyone down with you. When you focus on the things that are *not* happening, you create more stress for yourself and those around you.

Get your focus onto what you *want* to happen. Instead of praying, "Lord, please help my husband to stop ignoring my needs," start praying, "Lord, thank You for giving me my husband; please help us learn how to meet each other's needs." Keep your attention on what's good and holy rather than what's broken and sinful. As Philippians 4:8 says, "Summing it all up, friends, I'd say you'll do best by filling your minds and meditating on things true, noble, reputable, authentic, compelling, gracious—the best, not the worst; the beautiful, not the ugly; things to praise, not things to curse."

three things to do

Here are three things you can do to help make your marriage happier through the power of a positive mind. We've found that couples who are happy . . .

- know the value God places on them.
- shape their tomorrows by taking personal responsibility.
- envision and believe in a positive future.

Being made in God's image (Genesis 1:27), we humans have incredible value. None of His other creations got this distinction. We're capable of amazing things because we're made in the image of our Creator, who is good and holy.

When we take responsibility, we are helping to shape the future. This book is about using this power to help our marriage become stronger and more satisfying. For Christians, the Bible describes an even greater power. First John 5:4-5 says, "Every God-begotten person conquers the world's ways. The conquering power that brings the world to its knees is our faith. The person who wins out over the world's ways is simply the one who believes Jesus is the Son of God."

Maybe phrases like that have lost their luster with you, but that doesn't make them any less true! Take a husband and wife I (Amy) have been working with for over two years now. If you need help to believe in miracles, pay close attention to their story.

casey and sarah

They came to see me for a two-day intensive several years ago. The time went well, but Sarah was determined to leave Casey. There was nothing he nor I could say to help her understand the mistake she was making in leaving her husband. The intensive ended on a sour note because she would not commit to staying in the marriage.

I privately pulled Casey aside after we finished, encouraging him to stay focused on what could be and to give his wife over to God in prayer. I wanted him to believe their marriage could be restored and to put his faith and hope in Jesus by continuing to pray for his relationship and his bride.

For almost a year and a half Casey continued to pray and stay committed to his wife—even though she had decided to move out and even began dating another man!

Casey and I would talk on the phone; he would cry over what he was going through and how badly he wanted his wife back. It blew my mind to hear that he had put a note under each light switch in his home, every one containing the same word: PRAY.

Every time Casey flicked a light switch in his home, he was reminded to pray for his wife, his marriage, and restoration. He spent a year and a half praying for and about a wife who was unresponsive and hurtful.

> *Whatever is bringing your marriage down does not have to last forever.*

Then, one day, Casey got a phone call. It was Sarah. All she said was, "I want to come home."

These were the five words Casey had been praying for. That's 18 months of praying and hoping and believing that God could restore his wife and marriage!

They are back together again, working on their relationship.

Is there a lot that needs to be repaired and forgiven? Absolutely. But Casey gives all of us a great example of keeping focused on what really matters—and hanging in there even when it seems things will never work out the way we want them to.

getting your eyes fixed

When you focus on Jesus, you see and believe in a positive future. That's because you're fixing your eyes "not on what is seen, but on what is unseen. For what is seen is temporary, but what is unseen is eternal" (2 Corinthians 4:18, NIV).

Whatever is bringing your marriage down does not have to last forever. There are seasons in marriage when things feel worse. But they're seasons. If you're willing to wait, you can experience seasons of wonder as well. Just as "all good things must come to an end," so must the bad ones.

We were recently speaking at a family camp in Ohio, where a couple celebrating 59 years of marriage shared this very concept. The wife talked about how there had been valleys in their marriage, but that the valleys always led them to the mountaintops.

How will you ever experience the mountaintop if you constantly bail out in the valleys? Marriage is a journey—and not a short one, either. Journeys take time.

"But for right now, until that completeness, we have three things to do to lead us toward that consummation: Trust steadily in God, hope unswervingly, love extravagantly. And the best of the three is love" (1 Corinthians 13:13).

Stay positive, and choose love.

the miracle of the mirror

"Mirror, mirror on the wall, who's the fairest of them all?" How many books, movies, and plays echo these magical words uttered in Disney's *Snow White?*

Whether it's the looking-glass in *Snow White* helping the villainess destroy the beautiful heroine or the one in horror movies showing the monster about to kill the innocent person, mirrors never seem to be kind. Maybe you have your own mirror of horror at home reflecting the weight gained over years of eating more and exercising less.

Some people truly hate mirrors. They show our blemishes and our weaknesses. They're brutally honest, holding nothing back. If only they would be more sensitive and improve the way things look when we stare at them!

There's a good side to mirrors, though; they're honest. The only mirror that lies is one that's been tampered with. An unblemished mirror provides an accurate look at ourselves—including the things we may not want to see.

Early in our marriage I (Michael) struggled with Amy's *major* anger issues. Amy, as you learned earlier in the book, is an escalator. This means she struggles with yelling or "escalating" when her feelings get hurt or when her opinion differs from mine. I am the avoider, which means that I tend to withdraw or run away from conflict—and have a difficult time sharing my feelings and needs because I don't want to cause trouble.

I believed with all my heart that Amy had an anger problem. When she got upset, she *really* got upset. I would just look at her with puppy eyes, a tear running down my cheek, wondering how someone could have such a problem. I assumed that because I wasn't the one yelling or "freaking out," I was the victim of Amy's anger. I was an anger management snob!

I decided that my avoidance was far superior to her escalation. Thinking Amy needed help, I would frequently let her know just how "sick" she was! Immature and judgmental, I was completely unaware of my own anger issues. It never occurred to me that I might have as big a problem with anger as Amy did.

One day, while suffering through one of my major withdrawal periods when I wouldn't talk to her if my feelings had been hurt or I was otherwise upset, Amy walked by me in the kitchen.

"You know," she said, "when I'm avoided like this, it feels like the pain I'm experiencing is never going to end." She said it in such a calm and thoughtful manner that it hit me square in the nose (along with conviction from the Holy Spirit). I'd never realized before that moment how I had just as big an anger problem as Amy; I just showed it differently! Because Amy had not shamed me or come at me with a bad attitude, I was forced to see myself for who I really was—and my reflection in the mirror was very disappointing.

seeing yourself as others see you

What kind of miracle can a mirror produce for your marriage?

The miracle of the mirror was talked about in Scripture thousands of years ago. Romans 2:1 (NIV) teaches, "You, therefore, have no excuse, you who pass judgment on someone else, for at whatever point you judge the other, you are condemning yourself, because you who pass judgment do the same things."

This is a harsh beginning to Romans 2, because in Romans 1 Paul reveals all the disgusting and horrible things sinners do. We may applaud Paul and his condemnation of those things, but then he slams us hard to the ground! Suddenly we learn we're not better than those sickos! In fact, we're all sinful and fall short of the glory of God.

The miracle of the mirror is understanding that you're spiritually unhealthy, just like your spouse. This might come as a shock, especially if you've built quite the case against your mate. Maybe you've acted as judge and jury and your marriage is hurting as a result of your attitude. But when we judge our spouse (or anyone), we're really only lowering the boom on ourselves.

Judging is different from setting boundaries. It's different from confronting. Being judgmental includes a critical attitude toward your spouse; it's rude and self-centered. It doesn't care about the other person's feelings or needs, only about self. Boundaries, as Drs. Henry Cloud and John Townsend teach in their

> **When we judge our spouse, we're really only lowering the boom on ourselves.**

well-known series of books, are your ability to protect yourself from harm, not lashing out but keeping an open heart to reengage with your spouse. Confrontation is standing up for yourself as well, but keeps the rhetoric and name-calling out of the discussion; it's meant to increase intimacy. Being judgmental destroys that kind of closeness.

The Pharisees of Jesus' day practically wrote the book on being judgmental. How did Jesus feel about them? "Not good" is correct. At one point He called them a brood of vipers! That's not who we want to be.

When we acknowledge our own sinfulness, we're not degrading ourselves. We're merely admitting our faults. When we fully identify with the person staring back at us in the mirror, we confess to our own flaws. This can affect our marriage and our happiness, because we suddenly become more humble, patient, and understanding.

Acknowledging the mirror doesn't drag us down; it lifts us up!

The miracle is how we can become more understanding toward our spouse. This encourages him or her to be more open and intimate. And who doesn't want that in a marriage?

reflecting your spouse

The mirror concept can help your spouse take personal responsibility—if you're patient.

I (Amy) had a couple in conflict come into our office. The wife was getting after her husband and even attacking his personal appearance. He sat there and did not respond in kind. He did not repay evil for evil.

In doing this, he allowed her to see herself for who she was. The ugliness she dished out said more about her than he ever could. She was projecting her feelings onto him. Angry, she wanted to push him away; disliking herself, she lashed out at him.

> **The mirror concept can help your spouse take personal responsibility—if you're patient.**

By not pushing back, he became a mirror to his wife's flaws. She was left with evaluating her response, which was ugly.

Just minutes after she'd said all those nasty things, she backtracked: "You know, I really didn't mean that." It was the beginning of her taking responsibility for her words and actions. Because the husband hadn't reacted negatively to the wife's attack, she'd run out of ammunition. She was forced to see her own flaws because he didn't put any of *his* on display!

Words can hurt worse than a punch in the face. The wounds heal slowly, but the process is quickened when one person exercises the power of one—being patient, not sniping back, and becoming a mirror for the other spouse. This couple might not have gotten there had the husband counterattacked.

When you try to fight fire with fire, things only get worse. When you respond with prayer and a Christlike attitude, you lead your spouse to look in the mirror. He or she can't blame you for what appears there. Your mate may try, but if you give him or her nothing to cite in terms of your sin, all that's left is a reflection.

It takes discipline, but not returning harsh words works in the long run. It's okay to acknowledge that what your spouse said was hurtful. But then walk away and take a time-out until a more constructive conversation can take place.

take the first step

The miracle in the mirror begins with getting off our high horse and preparing our hearts to receive some of God's greatest gifts. Matthew 7:1-5 (NIV) spells it out:

> "Do not judge, or you too will be judged. For in the same way you judge others, you will be judged, and with the measure you use, it will be measured to you.
>
> "Why do you look at the speck of sawdust in your brother's eye and pay no attention to the plank in your own eye? How can you say to your brother, 'Let me take the speck out of your eye,' when all the time there is a plank in your own eye? You hypocrite, first take the plank out of your own eye, and then you will see clearly to remove the speck from your brother's eye."

Pastor Mark Driscoll of Seattle's Mars Hill Church delivered a sermon on this section of Scripture. He paraded around the platform holding a long two-by-four up to his eye. It was a great image (which we've stolen from time to time to make the same point to our audiences).

The problem with judging your mate isn't just that it decreases your overall marital satisfaction. The real trouble begins when the judging attitude comes right back at you. It's difficult to get grace from your spouse if you're unwilling to give it yourself.

Whatever you want from your spouse, take the initiative and offer the same to him or her. There's no time limit on how long you need to be forgiving, loving, kind, and patient.

Your job is to try to be like Jesus for the remainder of your life. No, you won't do it perfectly. But do it imperfectly, and you'll have the foundation of a happier marriage.

15

loving your spouse no matter what

One of the greatest love stories ever told is being lived, right now, by you.

We know your marriage may not feel like Romeo and Juliet's undying love or Tristan and Isolde's passion through unthinkable obstacles. But your story is just as bold and filled with as many twists and turns as any Jane Austen novel!

If you don't see your marriage as a great love story, pay close attention to this chapter. You might discover a romance greater than you imagined.

diamonds in the difficulties

The thing that makes a great love story is not the happy ending. Yes, we all love it when the guy gets the girl and they ride into the sunset together on a stallion. But that's not why we cry.

The Notebook was a touching movie because of the *difficulties*. *Romeo and Juliet* is arguably the greatest story ever written about love—because of the *tragedy*. True love stories have depth which can only be summoned through overcoming obstacles. To overcome is love; to rise above is love; to fall down and get back up is love; to die for each other is love.

I (Amy) have been meeting with a woman I'll call Julie Ann. Julie Ann's husband had an ongoing affair with a woman. He is not a believer, but Julie Ann is—a very committed one.

The average person would tell Julie Ann she's justified to divorce her husband and punish him for what he's done to her. But Julie Ann thinks differently. She came to me with her husband to get help. As I met with them I could see the genuine struggle toward healing he was having.

Is an ongoing affair reason enough to get divorced? It could be. Is Julie Ann's not standing up for her "right" to divorce a codependent move? Hardly. When you meet her and hear her conviction, when you hear his struggle and spend hours praying for her as she seeks God's will for her marriage, you get a different picture.

Julie Ann is not weak. In fact, she's faithful and strong. She would tell you her relationship with Christ is closer and has more depth than it did before her marital stress. The crisis that nearly destroyed her has only made her more committed to loving Christ and her husband. She believes her husband will begin a relationship with God through her commitment and faithfulness to their marriage and to Christ.

Your story is just as bold and filled with as many twists and turns as any Jane Austen novel.

She draws boundaries with her husband. They have learned how to communicate in a validating way. He is committed to being faithful to her and he shows his commitment in many different ways.

Julie Ann's greatest motive is to honor God. Yet she is human and often questions whether she is more committed to God or to the reward of a good marriage. It is this questioning and faithful pursuit that makes her so unique. We don't have enough Julie Anns in this world.

Maybe you're shaking your head in disbelief. But we wish you could meet Julie Ann! People with this kind of commitment and conviction are rare.

Sharing Julie Ann's story isn't meant to make you feel guilty if you've left a cheating spouse. The Bible is clear on what a believer can do when his or her spouse has an affair:

> "Why then," they asked, "did Moses command that a man give his wife a certificate of divorce and send her away?"
>
> Jesus replied, "Moses permitted you to divorce your wives because your hearts were hard. But it was not this way from the beginning. I tell you that anyone who divorces his wife, except for marital unfaithfulness, and marries another woman commits adultery." (Matthew 19:7-9, NIV)

The exception is marital unfaithfulness. So do you have the right to divorce a spouse who leaves his or her socks on the floor? No. Do you have the right to divorce a spouse who cheats on you? Yes. But do you *have* to? No.

This is where personal responsibility comes into play. When there's trouble in your relationship, you have to take on the work of finding out how God wants you to respond. Julie Ann has concluded—in a healthy way, we think—that God is calling her to stick with her marriage. She has spent hours in prayer and counsel. She didn't make this choice out of weakness, but from seeking God's will and having that affirmed through fellow Christians.

Julie Ann's story is not yet complete. Neither is yours. Read on to find out how love-based commitment and choice can help your epic romance turn out more happily.

a "choice" kind of love

"This is how much God loved the world: He gave his Son, his one and only Son. And this is why: so that no one need be destroyed; by believing in him, anyone can have a whole and lasting life" (John 3:16).

This verse is held up on signs at so many sporting events across the world because it personifies true love. It's at the center of Christianity because it poignantly speaks of the love God has for mankind. When someone lays down his life for your sake, you feel loved. There's no greater act of love than to give your life for someone.

If you're a Christ follower, you have the opportunity to be different. You have the opportunity to share in God's love and grow in the understanding of what love is truly about.

When you don't feel love for or from your spouse, God has the opening to overwhelm you. The emotional "block" you might be experiencing can only be unblocked by the eternal power of Christ. If we can lay down our sin and pride and desperately seek Jesus, He will be found. In Luke 11:9 (NIV) He says, "Seek and you will find."

Real love lasts; infatuation has a very short shelf life.

Urgently grabbing hold of God by studying His Word, seeking wise counsel, and connecting through worship will lead to a healing of your wounds only God can touch. By viewing your marriage crisis as a spiritual crisis, you invite God into your world in a very deep and powerful way.

Are you afraid God may ask you to do something your pride won't allow? Or are you afraid God may ask you to stand up for yourself?

You have an opportunity to "feel" loved by God. Our spouses will always fall short of God's love, but as Ephesians 3:17-19 (NIV) puts it, "And I pray that you, being rooted and established in love, may have power, together with all the saints, to grasp how wide and long and high and deep is the love of Christ, and to know this love that surpasses knowledge—that you may be filled to the measure of all the fullness of God."

The kind of love that survives the ages and becomes the stuff of fairy tales is a "don't give up" kind of love. It's a "choice" kind of love. It's not infatuation—those butterflies we get when first meeting the person we think we want to spend the rest of our lives with.

The difference between real love and infatuation is dramatic. Real love is based on a choice and makes any sacrifice. Infatuation is based on feeling and a "need" to be with each other night and day; it's an obsession, usually early in the relationship, when you constantly think of each other and feel blissfully happy to be together. Real love lasts; infatuation has a very short shelf life.

A happy marriage moves past infatuation (a transition which, for most couples, occurs shortly after the honeymoon) and toward unconditional love. The latter is tied not to circumstances but to decisions.

If you want to experience profound joy in your marriage, seek God's profound love first. The only way you can love no matter what is by experiencing the depth and wholeness of God's unconditional love for you.

God's love is unconditional, but it does hold us accountable for our actions. He wants us to be convicted but not condemned. "Therefore, there is now no condemnation for those who are in Christ Jesus" (Romans 8:1, NIV). Sometimes loving someone means you set boundaries on behavior. Drawing a distinction between loving the person and loving his or her behavior allows both of you to take ownership of your actions.

quitting time?

God never quits on us. What happens if we mess up over and over again? Like the drug addict, we just keep falling into the same stinking sin and can't seem to stop. But God doesn't say, "Look, I've tried to love you—I really have. But this problem of yours is too much for Me to handle. I love you; I just can't do it anymore."

Whoa! That statement sounds too familiar to us. We've heard this kind of rhetoric for years from people who gave up on their spouse because they felt it had been too long or they'd endured too many mistakes. We're not talking about people in abusive marriages, the kind described in the disclaimer at the beginning of this book.

We're talking about people who quit when quitting should not have been an option.

Quitting should never be an option when you're dealing with issues of communication or conflict resolution. Yet we've seen people divorce over problems that are truly solvable. Even an affair doesn't have to mean the end of your marriage. It might, but it doesn't have to.

If you're at your wit's end in your relationship, you may be wondering about your options. You need to seek answers through prayer, the Bible, a professional counselor, your pastor, and a community of believers.

Things don't always go as planned in life. Your spouse may have disappointed you, your child may be seriously ill, or your job may be gone. It might encourage you to see this comment one of our Facebook friends left us recently:

> Thought I'd share a quick bite of life in Topeka. I received a phone call this morning to let me know that I was being terminated from my position at work. As fate would have it, today is my wife's day off, and I got to tell her. Our first thought was "What do we do now?" [which] was immediately followed by the answer—"The same thing we always do: give thanks, bond together, and move forward."
>
> It's obviously a signal that, career-wise, something better is waiting for me. Much easier to handle crises when handled by more than one person! We have a sign above our door that says, "We may not have it all together, but together we have it all." Words to live by! Have a great day!

Every one of us should hang signs like that over our doors, declaring, "We may not have it all together, but together we have it all." Our marriages need that kind of staying power and sticking together and not giving up.

God never stops loving us. Even though we constantly mess up,

God never leaves nor forsakes us. His love is unconditional, and we need to follow His lead when it comes to loving our spouse. Quitting only eliminates our chance of truly experiencing real love.

That's the kind of love that has depth, the kind Romeo and Juliet were willing to die for. Love is not happiness, it's a choice. It's not a feeling, it's a decision. Love is endless, a no-matter-what kind of attitude!

Romans 5:8 (NIV) reads: "But God demonstrates his own love for us in this: While we were still sinners, Christ died for us." There were no preconditions.

God never says, "If you would only stop (insert your own issues here), I would finally be able to love you." *If you would only stop lying. And cheating. And being argumentative. If you would only stop invalidating and avoiding. If you would only . . .*

Thanks be to God for not having any *ifs* in His love for us. He loves us unconditionally, so let's return the favor to our spouse.

> **We've seen people divorce over problems that are truly solvable.**

You may be thinking, "Sure, but God loves us from a distance. He doesn't have to share a house, bed, and bank account with the jerk I'm married to!"

If this is true of you, we're sorry that you're hurting so much in your marriage. It's a great sorrow to be in a marriage where you feel rejected and ignored.

But God doesn't love you "from a distance." He's close enough to know your deepest pain. He chose to deal with your sin and pain when He sent Jesus to die on the cross. God is fully invested in your life and wants only the best for you.

If the person you're married to is being a jerk, what can you do about it? Would leaving the jerk suddenly make him or her less jerky? Probably not. In fact, most divorced people will tell you that their ex-spouse got *worse* after the divorce! Divorce is not the solution to a jerky spouse; it makes things even messier.

Romans 8:38-39 motivates us by declaring, "I'm absolutely convinced that nothing—nothing living or dead, angelic or demonic, today or tomorrow, high or low, thinkable or unthinkable—absolutely nothing can get between us and God's love because of the way that Jesus our Master has embraced us."

Do you hear God's love for you? If so, do your actions and attitude toward your spouse reflect it?

If you really want to know how to love your spouse, meditate on this famous chapter from the New Testament. It contains perhaps the most recognizable words on love ever written, even in this paraphrase from *The Message*:

If I speak with human eloquence and angelic ecstasy but don't love, I'm nothing but the creaking of a rusty gate. If I speak God's Word with power, revealing all his mysteries and making everything plain as day, and if I have faith that says to a mountain, "Jump," and it jumps, but I don't love, I'm nothing. If I give everything I own to the poor and even go to the stake to be burned as a martyr, but I don't love, I've gotten nowhere. So, no matter what I say, what I believe, and what I do, I'm bankrupt without love.

Love never gives up.

Love cares more for others than for self.

Love doesn't want what it doesn't have.

Love doesn't strut,

Doesn't have a swelled head,

Doesn't force itself on others,

Isn't always "me first,"

Doesn't fly off the handle,

Doesn't keep score of the sins of others,

Doesn't revel when others grovel,

Takes pleasure in the flowering of truth,

Puts up with anything,
Trusts God always,
Always looks for the best,
Never looks back,
But keeps going to the end.

Love never dies. Inspired speech will be over some day;
praying in tongues will end; understanding will reach its limit.
We know only a portion of the truth, and what we say about
God is always incomplete. But when the Complete arrives, our
incompletes will be canceled.

When I was an infant at my mother's breast, I gurgled
and cooed like any infant. When I grew up, I left those infant
ways for good.

We don't yet see things clearly. We're squinting in a fog,
peering through a mist. But it won't be long before the
weather clears and the sun shines bright! We'll see it all then,
see it all as clearly as God sees us, knowing him directly just as
he knows us!

But for right now, until that completeness, we have three
things to do to lead us toward that consummation: Trust
steadily in God, hope unswervingly, love extravagantly. And
the best of the three is love. (1 Corinthians 13:1-13)

staying power

It's easy to stay committed to your spouse when he's loving, caring,
thoughtful, and supportive. But what do you do when he messes up,
and we mean *really* messes up?

When the extramarital affairs of golfer Tiger Woods were revealed
in 2009, we wrote several posts on www.gosmalley.com about the situation. One post stands above the rest—because of a comment a
reader left. Here's a summary of what he wrote:

I had a story just like Tiger Woods. On the outside, I was doing great with a wonderful family, a full-time ministry position, active in our local church and community.

But I had a secret life just like Tiger. Without going into detail, my ministry leadership found out and fired me. I had to confess to my pastor, a deacon, my wife, and our family. I needed to get clinical help, spiritual counsel, and total accountability.

My dear wife stayed with me and her fears were enormous. There was nothing she could have done differently. She was and is a wonderful wife. After 24 years of marriage, [a marriage] she felt was a lie, she chose to stay with me.

Where are that man and his wife today? They're happily married and back in full-time ministry! God can do amazing things if you allow His influence in your life. In this case, the key was that the wife stuck with her husband against impossible odds, and the two of them reached out and got help.

It's not enough to just stick together, though. If you want things to *get* better, then you have to *become* better and see what happens next. Personal responsibility is the path to creating the best environment for your marriage to succeed.

That can start with you. Whether the problem you face is infidelity, lack of communication, or just a spouse who forgets your anniversary, you can't control him or her—but you can control whether you respond in love.

16

when your spouse
lets you down

I (Michael) was so excited about my little plan!

We were with our kids in Scottsdale, Arizona, doing a seminar for a church. Since I grew up in that area, it was sort of a homecoming for me. I was in such a good mood; the seminar went well, which means there was loud laughter. We were headed out to eat; the kids chose Maggiano's Little Italy. Being the great husband that I am—

Just a minute. Amy is interrupting this story to bring you the following important information!

Okay, I will admit that Michael is a great husband. I couldn't be more happy to be married to him. But don't let him fool you with the beginning of this story! Just hang in there to see how "great" he really was that evening in Scottsdale. Now back to Michael.

As I was saying, being the great husband that I am, I had pulled up to the front of the restaurant to drop off my wife and kids so they wouldn't have to walk all the way from where I could park the car. Amy thanked me for being so gracious, awesome, loving, adorable, and sexy (okay, maybe not adorable, but the rest of those words apply).

As I headed around the corner to park, I noticed there was a Capital Grille. If you've never eaten there, you have not experienced life! I could remember a time when I was truly happy—having the macaroni and cheese with lobster at that restaurant. (I think my weight gain during the last 15 years may have something to do with the fact that most of my favorite memories revolve around food! But this chapter is not about that; it's about what I did next.)

After parking the car, I had to walk past the Capital Grille. My mouth started watering. Then a big, brilliant idea popped into my head. I thought, *One of the greatest dinners you and Amy have ever eaten took place at a Capital Grille. Go in there, order some of that lobster with mac and cheese, and bring it into Maggiano's for your wife!*

Minutes later I came parading into Maggiano's with my "world-famous" lobster-mac-and-cheese in a to-go bag. Amy will never forget that moment, but not because it was a good one to remember.

> **Hope. Believe there is a chance things will change.**

You see, Amy's expectation in our marriage was that I would never humiliate or mortify her in public. That night destroyed her expectation! I had no idea it was considered rude to bring food from another restaurant. To make matters worse, the waiter serving us was taking drink orders at our table when I arrived with the bag.

I think I'd better turn this over to Amy now . . .

I was humiliated the moment I saw Michael making his way toward our table. Can you imagine your husband parading through a restaurant with a goofy smile on his face, carrying a bag of food from a competitor?

I tried to hide under the table, but it was too late. Michael had seen us and made a beeline in our direction. I couldn't believe he was bringing food from another restaurant. There is no dish on this planet I would ever want brought into a competitor's establishment; yet there he was, lobster-mac-and-cheese and all.

When I told him to put the bag under the table, he had the nerve to ask me why. He honestly couldn't understand what my problem was. He was clearly not embarrassed by his actions, and had difficulty validating me for mine. We almost started to get into World War III;

fortunately, we called a time-out and kept the dinner free of exploding emotions and unmet expectations.

when you're expecting

How do you handle it when your spouse doesn't meet your expectations? Couples all over the world have asked us if it's wrong to expect anything from a spouse. The answer is no, but it depends on what you're expecting.

Everyone has expectations about everything. Eliminating them would be unrealistic and impossible. The problem with expectations comes when reality fails to measure up. The more disappointed we are when that happens, the more negatively we tend to react. Continued frustration from unmet expectations can lead to anger, contempt, and despair.

What *should* we do when our spouse fails to meet our expectations? Hope. Believe there is a chance things will change. Don't give up. Romans 5:2-5 (NIV) has something to say about hope:

> . . . And we rejoice in the hope of the glory of God. Not only so, but we also rejoice in our sufferings, because we know that suffering produces perseverance; perseverance, character; and character, hope. And hope does not disappoint us, because God has poured out his love into our hearts by the Holy Spirit, whom he has given us.

When we open ourselves to the power of God, we begin to experience the change we so desperately want and need. We continue to believe in that power by staying connected to God. When you put your hope in God, you will find hope; when you trust in Him, you will find trust.

Expectations aren't wrong in themselves. But unrealistic ones—like thinking that your husband would never embarrass you by bringing a competitor's food into a restaurant—get you in trouble. I (Amy) now understand that because Michael and I are so different, there's no way he will stop embarrassing me. My hope these days is that he won't do the same thing twice!

I know I do things that bug him, too. Today our expectations of each other aren't that we won't make mistakes, but that we'll recognize when we've blown it and try not to do that again.

key #1: know what you expect

There are two keys to developing healthy, more responsible expectations. Both are important for engaged and married couples.

First, *be aware* of your expectations. Many engaged couples never discuss what they expect about things like time together, sexual frequency, vacations, socializing, diet, shopping, children, finances, cleaning, household repairs, and gender roles. Many married couples never discuss these things, either!

> **The more in the dark you are about each other's expectations, the more conflict you'll experience.**

If you're going to have healthy expectations, let each other know what's assumed in the relationship. The more in the dark you are about each other's expectations, the more conflict you'll experience.

When you begin sharing your expectations, you hear them out loud. This helps you adjust those that don't "sound" good. For example, if you expect to spend 10 hours a week on dates and other time together, that may be unrealistic. If you have children or a job, 10 hours a week is a hard standard to meet. Talk about what might be more realistic. Going on a weekly date night, for instance, is realistic (and very important). Four dates a week probably is unrealistic (even though it sounds really fun!).

Let's take expectations about sexual frequency as another example. Have you ever discussed with your spouse how many times in a month you would enjoy having sex together? If not, you'd better! Couples need to discuss this issue with each other because hurt feelings can really pile up when it involves sexual intimacy.

Do you know how many times the average couple has sex in a month? What would be your guess? Once? Twice? Two hundred and seventy-five? (Michael wanted to add that possibility.)

> Researchers don't all agree on how often the average couple has sex. According to *Understanding Human Sexuality* by Janet Shibley Hyde and John D. DeLamater (McGraw-Hill, 1997), the largest percentage of married couples reporting in a study said they had intercourse three times a week. But as an article on the MayoClinic.com Web site points out, "Statistics on sexual behavior can be quite misleading. For example, a couple might read that the average married couple has intercourse three times a week. They may not be aware, however, that this average includes a wide range. The frequency of intercourse might range from zero for some to 15 or 20 times a week for others. Therefore, even if their frequency of intercourse is more or less than three times a week, their behavior is within the range of normal human experience."[1]

The point is this: Be fair when it comes to expectations about sex. If you expect to have sex once every two months, that might not be fair. If you feel entitled to have sex eighteen times a month, that might not be fair, either (sorry, guys). When it comes to expectations, avoid taking a selfish stance. You want to hear the feelings and needs of your spouse and try to meet them.

Take time tonight or tomorrow to discuss your expectations with each other. Make sure you're aware of your assumptions about the more important elements in your life and marriage.

key #2: get real

Sharing your expectations with each other isn't enough. You must be willing to *make them realistic*. Real-world expectations are important because they set you up to succeed. Unhealthy or unfair expectations set you up to be hurt and frustrated with each other.

Sometimes you can come up with realistic expectations simply by discussing them. Whenever you disagree on what's realistic, work hard to validate each other before you try to solve your differences. Remember reading about validation earlier in this book? Now is a great time to use that new skill.

Remember, too, that if you have a relationship with God you're not alone in tackling the problem of expectations. Jesus says in John 16:33, "I've told you all this so that trusting me, you will be unshakable and assured, deeply at peace. In this godless world you will continue to experience difficulties. But take heart! I've conquered the world."

Jesus has ultimately won the battle, so take it easy if you come up against a wall of disagreement. Take your time to study the wall, and build a strategy together for dismantling it. When President Ronald Reagan uttered his famous words, "Mr. Gorbachev, tear down this wall!" it took the entire world community to figure out a way to open up all of Germany again.

The same is true for your marriage when you run into a wall of differences. If your expectations are too far apart and you can't figure out a way to bridge the gap, seek help. That can come in the form of a friend, marriage mentor, pastor, or counselor. Keep working on the issue until you reach agreement in the area in which you got stuck.

Realize, though, that your spouse may never meet your expectations fully. We live in a fallen, broken world, and bad things happen. Feelings get hurt; expectations go unmet. It may help to consider the apostle Paul's observation in Philippians 4:11-12:

Actually, I don't have a sense of needing anything personally. I've learned by now to be quite content whatever my circumstances. I'm just as happy with little as with much, with much as with little. I've found the recipe for being happy whether full or hungry, hands full or hands empty.

True happiness lies in a relationship with Jesus. It's important to develop healthy expectations and to be honest about them with your spouse. But because the world isn't perfect, it's also important to be content with very little or very much. Life is about learning how to be okay despite whatever is going on around you—which is a powerful form of taking personal responsibility for your reactions.

Even if your spouse doesn't choose to help meet your expectations, you can still be okay.

Expectations need to be known and shared with your spouse. Whether or not he or she chooses to meet them is out of your control. But be encouraged! Even if your spouse doesn't choose to help meet your expectations, you can still be okay. It doesn't have to mean the end of your world.

the best possible spouse

We believe you want a happy marriage, and that you can experience one. But a happy marriage is not guaranteed, no matter how you deal with expectations.

Maybe you're thinking, *This book promises a way to have a stronger marriage. But now I find out that you need to be content no matter what your marriage is like—and find happiness in your relationship with Jesus. Why did I bother to read this?*

You're bothering with this book because when you change yourself, your marriage is changed! You can't control your spouse, but you can influence him or her. What choice do you have, other than becoming the best possible spouse? Is behaving angrily and hatefully going to change things for the better?

Some couples come to our marriage intensives with poor attitudes. Their expectations aren't being met, but their poor reactions only make things worse. The worse they act, the worse things get. Personal responsibility can help them do the right thing in order to give their relationship a fighting chance.

What can you do when your spouse lets you down? You can respond well by living out the life God has called all of us to live. Instead of depending on your mate for happiness, you can put your trust in the One who doesn't disappoint—and learn contentment by keeping your expectations down-to-earth.

don't miss a good thing

This is going to be a short chapter.

It's not short due to insignificance, but because it's straightforward. It's about a no-nonsense concept that doesn't take a lot of words to explain.

In fact, the title alone is nearly enough to say it all!

what if it works?

Is your spouse not exactly what you'd hoped for? We assume you were in love when you first met, but has the fire faded because of neglect or disappointment?

Has your spouse been hurtful for many years through cruel words or lack of loving actions? Have you been embarrassed, humiliated, ignored, neglected, and generally wiped out by the actions of your mate?

Maybe the only thoughts you have about your marriage are, *Enough! I'm out! I can't handle this anymore!* Perhaps you even threaten a divorce or move out of the home.

Don't miss out on a good thing!

Divorce, not so good. Separation, not so good. Continued hurt, yuck! But what if your spouse responds to the power of one? What if your taking personal responsibility encourages him or her to make a change? What then?

When we urge you not to miss out on a good thing, we're saying that your spouse might actually change. If so, you need to be watching so that you don't miss the growth.

People do change. Sometimes we don't know how, but they do. Sometimes we don't know when, but they do. Sometimes we can't believe it's even possible, but they do.

Here are just a few things God uses to change people:
- books
- videos
- counselors
- pastors
- friends
- billboards
- Web sites
- magazine articles
- total strangers
- random acts of kindness
- trauma
- hurt
- evil
- advertising slogans
- license plates
- bumper stickers
- clouds
- rain
- sun
- wind
- storms
- a spouse who exercises personal responsibility
- basically anything that exists in this world

God uses some surprising things to help create an environment in which people can change and grow closer to Him.

Perhaps you've heard stories about amazing transformations—someone driving down the road in the throes of alcoholism, for instance, careening off the road and flipping the car, only to survive the accident, recommit to following Christ, and find healing from the addiction. This kind of stuff happens. We don't understand it; we can't wrap our minds around it. But it does happen.

There are simply too many stories like that to doubt this truth: People change because God is big and He promises to use for our good what tries to destroy us.

What if your spouse responds to the power of one?

Is there any limit to what God can do? One of our favorite questions to ask couples in our Marriage Restoration program is, "Do you believe a miracle could save your marriage?"

We typically ask this question when one spouse doesn't feel the marriage can be saved. When someone is at the bottom of the barrel of marital satisfaction, he or she can feel hopeless. But does he or she still believe in miracles?

This chapter is dedicated to miracles and keeping your heart open to the possibility of change.

open-heart surgery

We've had couples come to an intensive after being divorced for nine years! The stories we've heard during our fifteen years of working with marriages are incredible. We're not trying to give you false hope. We're trying to tell you to keep your heart open to God's limitless ability to affect your relationship!

We worked with a wife who'd been verbally and emotionally hurt for 10 years by her husband. For all those years he'd spent more time away from her than with her. He'd said mean things to wound her because of the pain in his own life. (One thing my [Michael's] father always taught me was that when people hurt you or say mean things, they're only doing it because they're in pain themselves.) This woman's husband didn't know how to do unto others any better than it had been done to him. It's not an excuse; it's just reality.

Finally, after 10 years of harsh language and unmet expectations, the wife told her husband Christmas morning that she was leaving him. It had been a particularly tough evening for her the night before, and she was finally done. She informed her husband that she wanted a divorce.

We are not recommending this approach; threatening divorce typically makes things worse. But it was the only option this woman felt she could use. And for this couple, it did make things worse for about 24 hours. But then God stepped in, using the husband's hurt and shock from his wife's announcement to wake him up to how horrible he'd been for all those years!

He made a complete 180-degree turnaround in his attitude and willingness to get help for their marriage. That's when they came to see us.

We wish we could tell you that this story had a happy ending, but it didn't. The wife was so bitter about the previous 10 years that she never reconnected with her husband. He was making all the right changes, doing exactly what we asked of him. He was growing as a Christian and beginning to attend a men's Bible study. He was present at home and taking care of their children. All the things the wife wished her husband would do during the previous 10 years of marriage were finally being done! It was exciting to see the change and growth in this man. He took a bad thing and used it to turn his life around.

People change because God is big and He promises to use for our good what tries to destroy us.

But the wife couldn't see it. Having allowed her anger to turn into bitterness, she refused to reopen her heart to the marriage. Even though her husband was quickly turning into the one she'd always wanted, she was missing it. Her feelings clouded her judgment and her vision.

This is why we tell people who've been wounded to build a boundary against the person who hurt them—making sure to leave a peephole in the wall. There's nothing wrong with protecting yourself against cruel and harmful people. But it's unwise not to build some sort of mechanism in your boundary to see if the person is changing.

be on the lookout

People do change. It's a fact of life. If your spouse has hurt you so much that you don't feel you can continue in the marriage, please keep open the possibility that eventually he or she may be different.

Two wrongs don't make a right. If someone is unloving to you, it's never okay to be unloving in return. A closed spirit is just as offensive as a hurtful one.

If you allow for the possibility of change in your spouse, you'll never regret it. Even if your spouse ends up leaving you, you won't regret doing the right thing. You never regret doing the right thing.

This doesn't mean you'll never hurt or feel let down. But you can be proud of the way you handled yourself, your actions, and your choices—the way you took personal responsibility.

Time is never wasted when you use it to honor God and others—including your spouse.

surprising solution scenarios

Now what?

This chapter presents some of the most common struggles we see couples facing today, then shows how to use the concepts of this book in those situations. We hope that if you're experiencing a similar issue, this will help you understand how *The Surprising Way to a Stronger Marriage* applies to the problem.

#1: fiscal therapy

Q: My wife is a spender and I'm a saver. How can I get her on a budget?

A: We have the opposite problem in our marriage. I (Michael) am the spender and Amy is the saver. But this is an issue for many couples.

The first thing you want to do is help your wife understand how her spending makes you feel. If you approach her by saying that her spending is out of control, things aren't going to go well for you. But if you tell her that when she spends this much money, you feel like a failure and powerless in the marriage, she'll be more willing to listen.

In this book we encouraged you to get off the facts and onto the feelings. It might help to go to our Web site at www.gosmalley.com/free-stuff and search for "core relational fears." This is our summary of the most powerful and common feelings people have over particular issues like spending and saving.

You give your marriage the best chance when you talk about feelings and not about facts. Forget talking about how much money is being wasted; those kinds of facts are always debatable, no matter what you think. So talk about feelings, and watch how your wife becomes more of an advocate and less of an enemy on spending.

Once your wife realizes how you feel about her spending, she probably will be far more willing to honor a budget. If you get stuck as you try to settle on a budget, call a time-out and get your small group (if you belong to one) or a counselor involved in helping the two of you come to an agreeable solution.

#2: the affair

Q: My husband has just admitted to an affair. How do I respond?

A: Some research suggests that a majority of couples will suffer from the effects of an affair. Estimates range from 40 percent to 60 percent![1]

If your spouse has had an affair, the first thing you need to do is take responsibility for your attitude and response. Your mate's sin is no excuse for you to berate him or her with hurtful words; don't allow your pain to spill over and make matters worse. Take a time-out and ask your spouse if he or she would be willing to seek help from a mentor, pastor, or marriage counselor. Trying to discuss an affair would be nearly impossible to do in a healthy way without a third party being involved.

We know you are hurting. We know you can't imagine how the marriage will ever survive the affair. But it can if you both make the right choices in response.

If your spouse refuses to go to counseling, then get help for yourself. You can experience positive change as a result of your spouse's hurtful actions against you.

You don't have to be a victim; you can be victorious if you give yourself the chance to heal. If you're a Christian, pray and connect with mature believers for the encouragement and support you need to get better.

An affair doesn't have to be the end of your marriage; it can be a beginning. God uses our messes to make us stronger, and your marriage can gain strength if you take care of your response and allow God to work on your spouse.

#3: you never take me anywhere

Q: My husband hasn't taken me out in years! How can I get him interested in a date night with me?

A: Date nights are a great way to maintain a satisfying relationship. But nagging, hassling, or complaining about a lack of dates isn't the solution.

If your husband is weak at planning these times together, take the initiative and plan them yourself. Where does it say that one spouse is responsible for planning the dates? We know it's nice to have a spouse who wants to plan and go on date nights, but if your mate is a lousy date nighter, you'll have to do the bulk of the planning.

Instead of complaining about how your spouse never plans a date, you can get out there and do it yourself. We don't mean to sound cruel, but it's the truth.

I (Michael) plan the vast majority of our dates. I grew up in a home where my parents went on lots of dates. Amy's parents didn't. They love each other very much, but date nights weren't important to them; consequently, they're not that important to Amy. But since Amy feels *I'm* important, when I plan a date she graciously comes with me and has a good time.

If you're planning *all* the date nights you could feel unimportant. I (Amy) don't want Michael to feel that way, so I show him his importance to me in other ways. If you feel unimportant or neglected, not going on date nights might be producing that feeling.

Address the issue of unimportance head-on. It's okay to ask your spouse to validate your feelings about not feeling cared for, or feeling you're low on his or her priority list. Date nights are investments in your relationship.

Michael and I set each other up to have great date nights by viewing them as a time to have fun together—only. We shake hands and decide not to fight or bring things up we know are hot topics for us.

You can tell your spouse, "I know sometimes we've gotten into arguments when we were on our date nights. I promise to enjoy our time as much as I can. I promise to not bring up hard topics on purpose. If either of us brings something up that we don't want to talk about, let's say it's okay to table it until after the date night." Now you've created an atmosphere that will be clear of conflict. It doesn't guarantee a great date night, but it sets the right tone.

#4: the tangled web

Q: My spouse has rekindled a friendship with an old flame through the Internet. She says there's no romance involved, but I'm starting to feel jealous and even betrayed. What do I do?

A: To the person who has the friendship:

Please acknowledge your spouse's feelings. Don't judge or criticize unless you want that in return. Ask the question, "Do you feel this relationship is more important than my relationship with you?" If the answer is yes, then say, "Help me understand how I am communicating that to you."

Then ask, "How can I show you that you're more important to me?" You may get answers like, "Stop communicating with that person," "Spend more time together," "Accept my feelings as valid," "Value who I am," or "Affirm me."

To the person who has a problem with the friendship:

Express your feelings as feelings, as in, "I feel betrayed, rejected, unimportant." This is not a time to lecture or criticize.

It's hard to do, but stick to your feelings versus proving your truth. You'll get much further with your spouse if you express how her actions are affecting your feelings. God designed us to care about each other; we need to get the message across in a way our spouse can receive.

So what happens if you get an answer like, "I don't care how you feel, I'm going to keep the friendship anyway"?

You just got hit below the belt. You back up, lower your boxing gloves, and say, "Wow, that really hurt. But I'm not going to punch back."

Then walk away, take a time-out, pray, regroup. If the problematic friendship continues, you'll need to seek out a third party—a small group, pastor, or counselor. It's okay for you to continue to want resolution.

Take a humble yet strong stance. A response like the following would convey openness as well as strength: "I could be blowing all this out of proportion. But I'm willing to listen and come up with a solution that meets both of our needs. Let's see if we can come to an understanding, then a solution. If we can't, no big deal; let's just talk to our small group about it next week." Don't make calling in a third party sound like an ultimatum, punishment, or "telling on" your mate.

#5: no trust fund

Q: What do I do when trust has been broken financially by my spouse?

A: You might need to set up some financial boundaries. It's okay to have separate bank accounts if trust has been lost financially. Your goal is to regain trust, but you may need some very serious limits before that can happen.

Please don't hide money unless you're in true physical danger. Deception is never a good option.

You'll need, in a calm moment, to find common ground and talk about your expectations and goals. Set up rules for both of you. Get practical with each other—asking, for example, "What do we really spend on groceries each month?"

Then set up consequences that will follow if problems recur. For instance, you might say, "Honey, I know we've talked about going on vacation or buying a new car. But we aren't saving enough to do that right now. Until we can, let's not look into doing those things now. If we can adjust and reach our goal of $_____ in the next three months, then I think we'll be ready to start planning again. What do you think?"

Do you see the "we"-ness of that conversation? It's not about one person punishing the other or one person being the saver and one the spender. The saver probably could go for a longer period without a new car or vacation, so why rush? What's more important is learning to be a united team.

#6: misery or miracle?

Q: I want a satisfying marriage, but I'm miserable. I want to do the right thing—like taking responsibility. But nothing has worked before, and I feel hopeless.

A: When I (Amy) don't know the answers to my questions I go back to a prayer I prayed in high school: "God, give me wisdom and understanding."

Solomon has been described as the wisest and richest man who ever lived. He seemed like a great person to pattern my life after (except for all those wives). He learned that asking for wisdom is like using a "buy one get three free" coupon. You ask for wisdom, but receive other valuable things, too.

Gaining wisdom helps me gain perspective. I like to think of wisdom as choosing to see the multiple layers of the human condition all around us. I want to see that reality so I can react in a way that might help someone else make a better choice. It's not my responsibility to change that person, but maybe I can influence him or her.

What if you ask God for wisdom where your spouse is concerned? Might you discover how to react in a way that helps him or her make better choices?

When I get bogged down in hurt, fear, or frustration, I ask for understanding:

- *What can I learn from this?*
- *Lord, what are You trying to grow in me?*
- *Do I need more humility, or a stronger sense of self-worth?*
- *Is this about me, or are You dealing mainly with my spouse?*

Perhaps asking questions like these will help you find what you're seeking, too.

Ultimately, what you're seeking is connection, love, and understanding. You may not get these things from your spouse—but you can from Jesus if you belong to Him. That may sound trite, but we're being honest.

We truly want you to find relief from your pain, and believe God grieves over your situation, too. But He allows pain so that growth can occur. And this particular pain may not last forever. I love this comment that a woman named Tracy posted on our Web site: "Remember, 'DON'T QUIT BEFORE THE MIRACLE HAPPENS!'"

Spiritual growth looks like Colossians 3:12 (NIV)—compassion, kindness, humility, gentleness, and patience. When you have these qualities it makes living with an unresponsive spouse a whole lot easier—because you recognize it's not all about you, and you're more connected to others and to God.

#7: past imperfect

Q: My spouse doesn't trust me. I had an affair years ago; when will the past stop affecting the future of our marriage?

A: The past does affect the present, but it doesn't destine an outcome. The more you want things to go back to the way they were, the harder and longer your fight for that will be. Things will *not* be the same, though, because you don't want the same result—an affair, a breach of trust.

Communicating feelings and needs without defensiveness, criticism, or shaming will foster openness and connection. If your spouse is doubtful and you try to "prove" his or her feeling wrong, feelings of hopelessness and guilt will creep in again.

If you validate the feeling, however, you can make progress. Try saying something like, "I understand that it's difficult for you to trust me. Is there anything I can do right now to help? Do you just want me to listen? Would you like to check my phone records, or something else? I want us to feel safe with each other. I don't want to be defensive every time this comes up. I think when this is brought up it makes me feel guilty again. I will try to not see you as punishing me but as wanting to feel safe again in our relationship."

#8: one at a time?

Q: I'm willing to seek help for our marriage, but my spouse isn't. What can I do?

A: Of the two of you, you're the one with the openness in this moment to hear what we're about to write. We'd be writing the same thing to your spouse if he or she were reading. But you are, so here we go.

The first thing to do is tell your spouse you're reading this book so you can be a better partner. You might want to say something like, "I understand you don't feel that asking for help will make a difference in our relationship. I want to understand why I feel stuck and how I can set up our marriage to be healthy and satisfying. I love and care for you. I want to understand you. I want our marriage to be the best it can be. I'm going to try to allow God's wisdom and guidance to humble me so that I'll be strong enough to love you in the most healthy way."

We're assuming, of course, that your marriage doesn't involve abuse. As we mentioned at the beginning of this book, we aren't calling on you to endure that. Sometimes the most loving and honoring thing you can do for someone is to stop him or her from mistreating you. Stopping abuse encourages growth and healing for both parties.

If you're the only one in your marriage who's willing to seek help, do so. A trained Christian therapist can assist you in charting a course that's most constructive for your relationship and for you personally.

#9: making it snappy

Q: I seem to be irritated all the time. My spouse drives me crazy. I snap too much at the person I'm supposed to care about most. I find myself shouting, then making excuses like, "If you hadn't been so immature, I wouldn't have *had* to yell." What can I do about this?

A: Welcome to my (Amy's) world. I have this tendency, too, and it's a thorn in my side that keeps me humbled.

May I share what I've done that helps me? First, I don't allow myself any excuses. On this issue I have a zero-tolerance policy with myself. I try to clean up every snappy act I do. I ask for forgiveness and tell Michael—or whoever I offended—that he or she didn't deserve my snappiness.

Second, I acknowledge the feelings underneath my anger. The usual suspects are fear, frustration, and hurt. By recognizing the more vulnerable emotions beneath my anger, I allow myself the opportunity to feel my true feelings. Anger feels powerful and protecting, but just behind the smoke and mirrors is a frightened and hurt person.

Third, I ask, "Is there anything I can do right now to repair our relationship?"

The person might name something I can do, and I respond accordingly. Or he or she might say, "No, I accept your apology. Thanks for asking."

Then I ask, "Are we okay, then?"

After that, I assume God's grace has covered me, and I get another chance to handle myself better next time.

If the person responds with, "I need time to think about what I need right now," I give him or her space and time to heal.

The bigger the hurt, the longer the time to heal. I can't force someone to accept my apology. My job is to be humble and ready to open up when the person is ready. It doesn't do either of us any good if I suddenly get mad again because the person needs more time.

My responsibility is to try to repair the damage by humbling myself before the person and God, and then to allow God's grace to be sufficient for me. I think the people closest to you should know that you're earnestly trying to take full responsibility for your temper. If you acknowledge the problem and don't try to push it off on them, they can offer grace more readily.

#10: don't start without me

Q: What if your spouse buys a car, boat, vacation condo, or whatever without telling you? I'm really ticked right now, and don't know what to do about it.

A: Personally, I (Amy) would need to take a jog around the block to get as much energy out as possible. Then I would ask, *"What were you thinking?"*

Just kidding. I would try to stay calm and say, "Help me understand why you bought the car." (Keeping sentences short helps me avoid blaming and escalating.)

There might be a legitimate reason: "We have talked about buying this car and it was such a great deal and the guy pressured me into it."

Okay, I got an answer. But I'm still mad. Now what?

I hope I would say something like, "Michael, I'm so hurt that you would make such a huge purchase without me. I'm going to need some time to cool down and then we can talk. How about I go out for a while? You take the kids and we can talk tonight after they go to bed." Then I would take a time-out.

What if he says, "Oh, you are so self-righteous; you bought furniture last month without telling me"? What would he be doing? Blame-shifting.

Having just been influenced (or "poked," as I like to call it) to become really angry, what's the best-case scenario for me? To walk away—to avoid engaging in the fight.

Continue the time-out until after the kids go to bed. Then have your conversation, sharing only feelings and needs: "I feel betrayed." "I feel unimportant because my opinion doesn't seem to matter."

You can see where this is going. Stay away from "You, you, you" accusations. Concentrate on the personal responsibility of "I feel" statements.

epilogue

So, what next?

By now you're aware of how much influence you can have over your marriage by taking full responsibility for your actions and attitudes toward your spouse.

Can you change your spouse? No.

But can you change yourself? Yes.

When you change yourself and strive to be more like Christ, you create an opportunity for your spouse to change—and for your marriage to experience the happiness and strength you want so much.

I (Michael) met with a woman today whose husband had moved out. He refused to show up for the Marriage Restoration Intensive they'd paid for several months earlier. There's a no-refund policy, so the wife decided to come in anyway.

When she sat down in our office, she started crying. She didn't know what to do or how to respond to her husband's hurtful words and actions. I quietly listened, then encouraged her to believe that there's a *lot* she can do.

We met for several hours as I unpacked the principles in this book. At the end of our time she looked at me and said, "This is the first time in months that I've felt any kind of hope for my marriage."

Remember, she made this comment even though her husband hadn't shown up for the intensive! Why? Because she knew that no matter what her husband did from this point forward, she was going to make the right decisions and handle herself in a way that would honor both God and her husband.

She finally felt empowered. So can you!

Jimmy Valvano, former basketball coach at North Carolina State, became a household name in 1993 when he delivered a speech at ESPN's first annual ESPY Awards banquet. He was dying of cancer.

Weak from his battle, "Jimmy V" had to be helped up the steps of the stage so he could address the crowd.

Knowing his own death was imminent, he gathered his remaining strength—and delivered the speech of a lifetime. As it neared a close, he announced the formation of a foundation that would help raise money to find a cure for cancer. He told the silent crowd that this foundation might not find a cure fast enough to save him, but he left them with the following words:

> And its motto is, "Don't give up, don't ever give up." That's
> what I'm going to try to do every minute that I have left. I will
> thank God for the day and the moment I have.[1]

Those are the words we want to leave with you: *Don't give up.*

You have the power of one. You have access to God's power, too, through a relationship with His Son.

If the change in your marriage starts with you, there's no telling how far it may go.

But there's only one way to find out.

Study Guide

by Michael and Amy Smalley

Chapter 1—You've Got the Power

The Challenge

What can *you* do to improve your marriage? Take a look at your attitude in the last week. What tone did you set in your relationship?

Key Verses

Isaiah 42:7

"I have set you among my people to bind them to me,
    and provided you as a lighthouse to the nations,
To make a start at bringing people into the open, into light:
    opening blind eyes,
    releasing prisoners from dungeons,
    emptying the dark prisons."

2 Thessalonians 1:11

"Because we know that this extraordinary day is just ahead, we pray for you all the time—pray that our God will make you fit for what he's called you to be, pray that he'll fill your good ideas and acts of faith with his own energy so that it all amounts to something."

Questions

1. What's the quickest way for your marriage to get better?
2. Are you focused on your spouse's neglect? On his or her bad attitude? If so, how's that working for you?
3. Do you have a choice in how you respond to your spouse's attitude or tone? If so, what are your options?

Chapter 2—When the Truth Is Hard to Swallow

The Challenge

How have your actions affected your marriage? If you have a relationship with God, find a quiet place somewhere and ask the Holy Spirit to reveal to you things that you've done that negatively shaped your marriage. Then talk to your spouse about the results, asking forgiveness for what you believe was unproductive, unhealthy, or reflected a selfish attitude.

Key Verses

1 Kings 8:46
"When they sin against you—and they certainly will; there's no one without sin! . . ."

Luke 6:31
"Here is a simple rule of thumb for behavior: Ask yourself what you want people to do for you; then grab the initiative and do it for them!"

Philippians 4:8
"Summing it all up, friends, I'd say you'll do best by filling your minds and meditating on things true, noble, reputable, authentic, compelling, gracious—the best, not the worst; the beautiful, not the ugly; things to praise, not things to curse."

Questions

1. Are you ever truly innocent in conflict with your spouse? How would you describe your tone, nonverbal signals, and the way in which you're usually interpreted?
2. What happens to your marriage when you don't recognize your own faults?

3. What happens when you blame your spouse for the problems in your marriage?

Chapter 3—"It's Not My Fault!"

The Challenge
Take control of how you respond to your spouse's issues or hurts against you.

Key Verses
John 8:31-32

"Then Jesus turned to the Jews who had claimed to believe in him. 'If you stick with this, living out what I tell you, you are my disciples for sure. Then you will experience for yourselves the truth, and the truth will free you.'"

Genesis 3:12

"The Man said, 'The Woman you gave me as a companion, she gave me fruit from the tree, and, yes, I ate it.'"

Matthew 7:1-5

"Don't pick on people, jump on their failures, criticize their faults—unless, of course, you want the same treatment. That critical spirit has a way of boomeranging. It's easy to see a smudge on your neighbor's face and be oblivious to the ugly sneer on your own. Do you have the nerve to say, 'Let me wash your face for you,' when your own face is distorted by contempt? It's this whole traveling road-show mentality all over again, playing a holier-than-thou part instead of just living your part. Wipe that ugly sneer off your own face, and you might be fit to offer a washcloth to your neighbor."

Romans 14:13b (ESV)
"Decide never to put a stumbling block or hindrance in the way of a brother."

Questions

1. Have you and your spouse been blaming each other for conflicts in your marriage? If so, how can you point a finger back toward yourself?
2. Why do we like to blame our spouse so much?
3. Why is it arrogant to make excuses for our actions?

Chapter 4—Getting Off the Defense

The Challenge
Instead of trying to defend yourself, seek to understand your spouse's needs and feelings. Lay down your emotions for a moment, go to your mate, and ask him or her to describe the situation before you get defensive.

Key Verses
Proverbs 3:13-14 (NIV)
"Blessed is the man who finds wisdom,
the man who gains understanding,
for she is more profitable than silver
and yields better returns than gold."

Matthew 5:21-24
"You're familiar with the command to the ancients, 'Do not murder.' I'm telling you that anyone who is so much as angry with a brother or sister is guilty of murder. Carelessly call a brother 'idiot!' and you just might find yourself hauled into court. Thoughtlessly yell 'stupid!' at a sister and you are on the brink of hellfire. The simple moral fact is that words kill.

"This is how I want you to conduct yourself in these matters. If you enter your place of worship and, about to make an offering, you suddenly remember a grudge a friend has against you, abandon your offering, leave immediately, go to this friend and make things right. Then and only then, come back and work things out with God."

Questions

1. Why do we get defensive with our spouse? Could it have something to do with our own issues or guilt?
2. Does getting defensive ever help calm the situation down? Why not?
3. If defensiveness doesn't work with a spouse, what does?

Chapter 5—You Don't Have to Be a Victim

The Challenge
Instead of reacting to your spouse, try taking a time-out instead.

Key Verses
2 Corinthians 5:10
"Sooner or later we'll all have to face God, regardless of our conditions. We will appear before Christ and take what's coming to us as a result of our actions, either good or bad."

James 1:19-20 (NIV)
"My dear brothers, take note of this: Everyone should be quick to listen, slow to speak and slow to become angry, for man's anger does not bring about the righteous life that God desires."

Questions
1. Do you have a story like the one about our birthday card incident? What did you do after that to repair your relationship?

2. Do you agree that your spouse doesn't *make* you react the way you do, and that your response is a choice? Why or why not?

3. What's the first thing you can do to respond differently to your spouse when he or she has hurt you?

Chapter 6—Letting God Handle the Hard Stuff

The Challenge
Stop trying to change your spouse.

Key Verses
2 Timothy 2:24-25
"God's servant must not be argumentative, but a gentle listener and a teacher who keeps cool, working firmly but patiently with those who refuse to obey. You never know how or when God might sober them up with a change of heart and a turning to the truth . . ."

Romans 12:2
"Don't become so well-adjusted to your culture that you fit into it without even thinking. Instead, fix your attention on God. You'll be changed from the inside out. Readily recognize what he wants from you, and quickly respond to it. Unlike the culture around you, always dragging you down to its level of immaturity, God brings the best out of you, develops well-formed maturity in you."

Questions
1. What have you been trying to change in your spouse? How have your efforts been received?

2. Instead of fixing attention on our spouse, where does our focus need to be?

3. Do you think it would be important to build your own PIT Crew? Who would you want to include?

Chapter 7—Which Way Are You Leaning?

The Challenge
Instead of avoiding the hurt or conflict in your marriage, lean in toward each other—and toward God.

Key Verses
Matthew 6:14-15
"In prayer there is a connection between what God does and what you do. You can't get forgiveness from God, for instance, without also forgiving others. If you refuse to do your part, you cut yourself off from God's part."

James 1:2
"Consider it a sheer gift, friends, when tests and challenges come at you from all sides."

Questions
1. Is there something you need to forgive your spouse for, but haven't seemed able to? If so, what is it?
2. Why is it important to forgive your spouse?
3. What kind of attitude do we need to have if our spouse wrongs us?

Chapter 8—It's Never about the Facts

The Challenge
Instead of focusing on the facts of an argument, try to discover the feelings underneath the frustration or hurt.

Key Verses

Proverbs 11:2 (NIV)
"When pride comes, then comes disgrace,
but with humility comes wisdom."

Psalm 37:11 (NIV)
"But the meek will inherit the land
and enjoy great peace."

Proverbs 27:17
"You use steel to sharpen steel,
and one friend sharpens another."

Questions

1. What truly matters in a marriage when conflict erupts?
2. Why does focusing on facts create disharmony?
3. If most conflict isn't about "truth," what is it about?

Chapter 9—Why Your Spouse
Is Always Right

The Challenge

Try putting your own concerns aside this week and validate your
spouse, especially if you're not feeling validated.

Key Verse

Ephesians 4:2-3 (NIV)
"Be completely humble and gentle; be patient, bearing with
one another in love. Make every effort to keep the unity of the
Spirit through the bond of peace."

Questions

    1. Instead of rushing to judgment against your spouse, how could you respond differently next time you feel controlled or ignored?

    2. What happens to your spouse when he or she feels validated? Do things get worse or better?

    3. What keeps you from validating your spouse?

Chapter 10—Taking Time-outs

The Challenge

Perhaps by now you've practiced taking a time-out. Now take another one, looking inward to see how God lets you know where you need to change. Look to Christ to humble, strengthen, and mold you into who He wants you to be.

Key Verses

    Psalm 86:15

    "But you, O God, are both tender and kind,

    not easily angered, immense in love,

    and you never, never quit."

    Isaiah 40:31 (NIV)

    "But those who hope in the LORD

    will renew their strength.

    They will soar on wings like eagles;

    they will run and not grow weary,

    they will walk and not be faint."

Questions

    1. What's the most important thing for you to do during a time-out?

2. Who has an easier time calling a time-out—an escalator or an avoider? Why?

3. How does taking a time-out demonstrate love and personal responsibility?

Chapter 11—Correcting and Connecting

The Challenge
Try to change one negative belief about your spouse. Challenge it with a reality check. Practice extending grace to your mate in that area this week.

Key Verses
Romans 8:6 (NIV)
"The mind of sinful man is death, but the mind controlled by the Spirit is life and peace."

Psalm 106:25 (NIV)
"They grumbled in their tents and did not obey the LORD."

Ephesians 4:29
"Watch the way you talk. Let nothing foul or dirty come out of your mouth. Say only what helps, each word a gift."

Questions
1. What's so destructive about having negative beliefs regarding your spouse?

2. Why are clarifying questions so important to a happy marriage?

3. If you find out that you're holding negative beliefs about your mate, what should you do next?

Chapter 12—The Trillion-dollar Question

The Challenge

Instead of assuming you know what your spouse needs from you, ask the Trillion-dollar Question (TDQ) in the next three days. It might take one of these forms:

"What can I do to make this right?"

"What do you need from me at this moment?"

"How can I help you right now?"

"Is there anything you need from me?"

Key Verses

Matthew 5:48

"In a word, what I'm saying is, Grow up. You're kingdom subjects. Now live like it. Live out your God-created identity. Live generously and graciously toward others, the way God lives toward you."

Matthew 22:34-40

"When the Pharisees heard how he had bested the Sadducees, they gathered their forces for an assault. One of their religion scholars spoke for them, posing a question they hoped would show him up: 'Teacher, which command in God's Law is the most important?'

"Jesus said, ' "Love the Lord your God with all your passion and prayer and intelligence." This is the most important, the first on any list. But there is a second to set alongside it: "Love others as well as you love yourself." These two commands are pegs; everything in God's Law and the Prophets hangs from them.' "

Questions

1. Why is it important not to assume that we know what our spouse needs?
2. How could the TDQ help jump-start happiness in your marriage?
3. If your spouse asked you the TDQ, what kind of message would that send to you?

Chapter 13—The Power of the Positive

The Challenge
Choose this week to focus on the things your spouse is doing right.

Key Verses
1 John 5:4-5

"Every God-begotten person conquers the world's ways. The conquering power that brings the world to its knees is our faith. The person who wins out over the world's ways is simply the one who believes Jesus is the Son of God."

2 Corinthians 4:17-18

"These hard times are small potatoes compared to the coming good times, the lavish celebration prepared for us. There's far more here than meets the eye. The things we see now are here today, gone tomorrow. But the things we can't see now will last forever."

1 Corinthians 13:13

"But for right now, until that completeness, we have three things to do to lead us toward that consummation: Trust steadily in God, hope unswervingly, love extravagantly. And the best of the three is love."

Questions

1. Are you in charge of your own happiness, or are you dependent on what your spouse does or doesn't do?

2. What's one way in which you could see your spouse from a fresh, positive perspective this week?

3. Max Lucado writes, "Focus on giants—you stumble. Focus on God—your giants tumble." What "giants" in your marriage do you tend to focus on? What could happen if you focus on God instead?

Chapter 14—The Miracle of the Mirror

The Challenge

What are the key areas in *your* life that need attention? Work on those things and stop worrying about your spouse's issues.

Key Verses

Romans 2:1-2

"Those people are on a dark spiral downward. But if you think that leaves you on the high ground where you can point your finger at others, think again. Every time you criticize someone, you condemn yourself. It takes one to know one. Judgmental criticism of others is a well-known way of escaping detection in your own crimes and misdemeanors. But God isn't so easily diverted. He sees right through all such smoke screens and holds you to what you've done."

Colossians 3:12 (NIV)

"Therefore, as God's chosen people, holy and dearly loved, clothe yourselves with compassion, kindness, humility, gentleness and patience."

Matthew 5:7-9 (NIV)
"Blessed are the merciful,
      for they will be shown mercy.
Blessed are the pure in heart,
      for they will see God.
Blessed are the peacemakers,
      for they will be called sons of God."

Questions

1. Which of your spouse's issues do you need to "let go of" so that you can work on your own?
2. How do you feel when your spouse judges you? How do you think it makes your spouse feel when you judge?
3. If you focus on your own issues, how might your spouse respond?

Chapter 15—Loving Your Spouse No Matter What

The Challenge

Next time you're irritated at your spouse, choose love, patience, kindness, mercy, and grace. First, though, decide: How will these qualities probably look when the time comes?

Key Verses

John 3:16
"This is how much God loved the world: He gave his Son, his one and only Son. And this is why: so that no one need be destroyed; by believing in him, anyone can have a whole and lasting life."

1 John 4:8-11
"The person who refuses to love doesn't know the first thing about God, because God is love—so you can't know him if you

don't love. This is how God showed his love for us: God sent his only Son into the world so we might live through him. This is the kind of love we are talking about—not that we once upon a time loved God, but that he loved us and sent his Son as a sacrifice to clear away our sins and the damage they've done to our relationship with God. My dear, dear friends, if God loved us like this, we certainly ought to love each other."

Romans 8:38-39
"I'm absolutely convinced that nothing—nothing living or dead, angelic or demonic, today or tomorrow, high or low, thinkable or unthinkable—absolutely nothing can get between us and God's love because of the way that Jesus our Master has embraced us."

Questions
1. What are you willing to do for the sake of your marriage?
2. Does unfaithfulness necessitate divorce? Why or why not?
3. What's one way in which you can show your spouse Christ's love for you?

Chapter 16—When Your Spouse Lets You Down

The Challenge
Make sure the expectations you have for your spouse are fair. If stress in your marriage makes it hard to evaluate your expectations, ask a mentor, pastor, friend, or counselor to help you.

Key Verses
Romans 5:2-5 (NIV)
"Through whom we have gained access by faith into this grace in which we now stand. And we rejoice in the hope of the glory of God. Not only so, but we also rejoice in our sufferings,

because we know that suffering produces perseverance; perseverance, character; and character, hope. And hope does not disappoint us, because God has poured out his love into our hearts by the Holy Spirit, whom he has given us."

John 16:33
"I've told you all this so that trusting me, you will be unshakable and assured, deeply at peace. In this godless world you will continue to experience difficulties. But take heart! I've conquered the world."

Philippians 4:11-12
"Actually, I don't have a sense of needing anything personally. I've learned by now to be quite content whatever my circumstances. I'm just as happy with little as with much, with much as with little. I've found the recipe for being happy whether full or hungry, hands full or hands empty."

Questions
1. Have you ever shared with your spouse your expectations about time together, sexual frequency, or romance? If not, please do so now.
2. What are three things you'd like to stop in your marriage?
3. What are three things you'd like to start?

Chapter 17—Don't Miss a Good Thing

The Challenge
Are you missing out on a good thing? Be open to noticing even the smallest positive change in your spouse's behavior or actions toward you.

Key Verses

Matthew 8:13 (NIV)

"Then Jesus said to the centurion, 'Go! It will be done just as you believed it would.' And his servant was healed at that very hour."

Mark 9:23 (NIV)

" 'If you can?' said Jesus. 'Everything is possible for him who believes.' "

Questions

1. What are some good things you can say about your spouse and marriage?
2. What needs to happen in your marriage for change to begin?
3. To whom can you turn in times of hurt or frustration to give you guidance and hope? What role would you like God to play in that process? Who might be able to help you find human comforters and counselors as well?

Chapter 18—Surprising Solution Scenarios

The Challenge

Compare conflicts in your marriage to the cases described in this chapter. Then, based on the advice offered, decide how to apply the principle of personal responsibility to your situation.

Key Verses

James 1:22-24

"Don't fool yourself into thinking that you are a listener when you are anything but, letting the Word go in one ear and out the other. Act on what you hear! Those who hear and don't act are like those who glance in the mirror, walk away, and two minutes later have no idea who they are, what they look like."

Proverbs 15:22
"Refuse good advice and watch your plans fail;
take good counsel and watch them succeed."

Questions
1. Which of these scenarios comes closest to one you face in your own marriage?
2. Which parts of the solution make the most sense to you? Which are you unsure of? Which chapter in the book might help most if you reread it?
3. What role does "the power of one" play in your solution? How will it help to take responsibility for your own feelings and actions?

notes

Chapter 1

1. If you haven't heard about our MRI program, go to http://smalley.cc/hope to learn more. In brief, an MRI is a one-day or two-day counseling experience in which couples from all over the country come to Houston, Texas. The intensive format is extremely successful in helping couples in crisis turn their marriages around, stay together, and increase their overall marital satisfaction.
2. "Five-Year-Old Girl Found After a Month," Associated Press, January 25, 2005, found at www.msnbc.msn.com/id/6862983.
3. Joe White with Lissa Halls Johnson, *Sticking with Your Teen* (Focus on the Family/Tyndale House Publishers, 2006), pp. 117-118.

Chapter 3

1. Found at http://www.desiringgod.org/Blog/Author/33_ben_reaoch.
2. Widiger, T.A. and Sanderson, C.J., "Personality Disorders Affect 10-15 Percent of the Adult U.S. Population," *Psychiatry* (Philadelphia: Harcourt Brace & Co., 1997), pp. 1291-1317.

Chapter 8

1. Found at http://pastors.crossmap.com/article/blessed-are-the-meek/item331.htm.

Chapter 10

1. Drs. Howard Markman, Scott Stanley, and Susan Blumberg, *Fighting for Your Marriage* (San Francisco: Jossey-Bass, 2001).

Chapter 13

1. Found at http://en.wikipedia.org/wiki/Logotherapy.

Chapter 16

1. Phillip J. Swihart, Ph.D., and Wilford Wooten, eds., *Complete Guide to the First Five Years of Marriage* (Carol Stream, Illinois: Tyndale House Publishers/Focus on the Family, 2006), p. 158.

Chapter 18

1. Janis Abrahms Spring, Ph.D. and Michael Spring, *After the Affair: Healing the Pain and Rebuilding Trust When a Partner Has Been Unfaithful* (New York: Harper Paperbacks, 1997).

Epilogue

1. Found at http://www.jimmyv.org/remembering-jim/espy-awards-speech.html.

FOCUS ON THE FAMILY®

Welcome to the Family

Whether you purchased this book, borrowed it or received it as a gift, we're glad you're reading it. It's just one of the many helpful, encouraging and biblically based resources produced by Focus on the Family® for people in all stages of life.

Focus began in 1977 with the vision of one man, Dr. James Dobson, a licensed psychologist and author of numerous best-selling books on marriage, parenting and family. Alarmed by the societal, political and economic pressures that were threatening the existence of the American family, Dr. Dobson founded Focus on the Family with one employee and a once-a-week radio broadcast aired on 36 stations.

Now an international organization reaching millions of people daily, Focus on the Family is dedicated to preserving values and strengthening and encouraging families through the life-changing message of Jesus Christ.

Focus on the Family MAGAZINES

These faith-building, character-developing publications address the interests, issues, concerns, and challenges faced by every member of your family from preschool through the senior years.

For More INFORMATION

ONLINE:
Log on to
FocusOnTheFamily.com
In Canada, log on to
FocusOnTheFamily.ca

PHONE:
Call toll-free:
**800-A-FAMILY
(232-6459)**
In Canada, call toll-free:
800-661-9800

THRIVING FAMILY™
Marriage & Parenting

**FOCUS ON
THE FAMILY
CLUBHOUSE JR.®**
Ages 4 to 8

**FOCUS ON
THE FAMILY
CLUBHOUSE®**
Ages 8 to 12

**FOCUS ON
THE FAMILY
CITIZEN®**
U.S. news issues

Rev. 4/10

More Great Resources
from Focus on the Family®

Your Spouse Isn't the Person You Married: Keeping Love Strong Through Life's Changes
By Teri K. Reisser, M.F.T. and Paul C. Reisser, M.D.
Using candid insights, humor, and stories drawn from years of experience, the Reissers show how to prevent and repair marriage rifts that develop with time. Recapture intimacy and grow closer to your spouse—not further apart.

Happily Ever Laughter: Discovering the Lighter Side of Marriage
Ken Davis, General Editor
God proved His sense of humor by inventing marriage. He also proved that two radically different, shockingly incompatible, deeply flawed people can actually become one. You'll rediscover that truth as you smile your way through these pages.

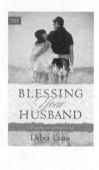

Blessing Your Husband: Understanding and Affirming Your Man
By Debra Evans
Your thoughts, words, attitudes, and actions help shape the man you married. By understanding his unique characteristics, how he thinks, and what matters most to him, you'll build a relationship that's more satisfying to both of you.